T0068214

LIVE *and* LET LIVE

SEEKING EMOTIONAL SOBRIETY

Doug S.

WESTBOW
PRESS®
A DIVISION OF THOMAS NELSON
& ZONDERVAN

WestBow Press books may be ordered through booksellers or by contacting:

WestBow Press
A Division of Thomas Nelson & Zondervan
1663 Liberty Drive
Bloomington, IN 47403
www.westbowpress.com
844-714-3454

ISBN: 978-1-6642-5689-7 (sc)
ISBN: 978-1-6642-5691-0 (hc)
ISBN: 978-1-6642-5690-3 (e)

Library of Congress Control Number: 2022902144

Print information available on the last page.

WestBow Press rev. date: 02/09/2022

For my wife, Joan.

Since defective relations with other human beings have nearly always been the immediate cause of our woes, including our alcoholism, no field of investigation could yield more satisfying and valuable rewards than this one.
—*Twelve Steps and Twelve Traditions,* Alcoholics Anonymous World Service, Inc.

Contents

Introduction

I am a Christian. I serve my Savior Jesus Christ, worship my Creator God, and rely on comfort, guidance, and discipline from the Holy Spirit. I am also a recovering alcoholic. I have not drunk alcohol or used mind-altering substances since July 1, 1985. I owe my sobriety to God's mercy and the program of Alcoholics Anonymous. If you or someone you know is struggling with addiction, I pray you will find a solution. Without a solution, it is impossible to live the life intended for you by your Creator. But what about those who have been released from the bondage of drugs and alcohol but still are unable to enjoy the fruits of authentic relationships?

The purpose of this book is to explore what is left for an addict to do after the compulsion to drink or use has been removed. To be freed from the bondage of those substances is a lifesaving and life-transforming miracle. My personal journey is chronicled in my first book, *Spiritual Awakening,* by Will Power (pen name). The book described the way it was, what happened, and a lot of the way it is today. I also described what happened to be delivered from addictions to work, shopping, and lust (sex). Here are the steps I took:

> - admission of a problem
> - coming to believe that a Higher Power could help
> - deciding to rely on that power for help
> - owning up to my character defects
> - admitting the exact nature of my wrongs
> - seeking removal of character defects
> - making amends to those who were harmed

- ➤ a daily review to correct harm done
- ➤ seeking and doing God's will
- ➤ helping other alcoholics
- ➤ behaving better

All the elements listed may not be required for everyone's path to recovery, but they are core to my solution. I have been blessed to be a member of Alcoholics Anonymous and have reaped the promises afforded those who do the work. First and foremost, I am still sober. I am proof that the program works. It really does.

> For by this time sanity will have returned. We will seldom be interested in liquor. If tempted, we recoil from it as from a hot flame. We react sanely and normally, and we will find that this has happened automatically. We will see that our new attitude toward liquor has been given us without any thought or effort on our part. It just comes! That is the miracle of it. We are not fighting it, neither are we avoiding temptation. We feel as though we had been placed in a position of neutrality—safe and protected. We have not even sworn off. Instead, the problem has been removed. It does not exist for us. We are neither cocky nor are we afraid. That is our experience. That is how we react so long as we keep in fit spiritual condition. *(Alcoholics Anonymous, 4th ed. (pp. 84–85), AA World Services, Inc.)*

Because I have had a spiritual awakening, I try to share the program with alcoholics and practice the AA principles in my daily living. I continue to go to AA meetings and render service regularly. I am happy to do these things as my life in sobriety is the best possible life for me. I love AA and the people in it. I am grateful for my solution.

For some time though, I have been asking, "Is there anything more? "What more do I need to become emotionally sober?" Bill Wilson, one of the cofounders of AA, came to the same place in his recovery.

> I think that many oldsters who have put our AA "booze cure" to severe but successful tests still find they often lack

emotional sobriety. Perhaps they will be the spearhead for the next major development in AA—the development of much more real maturity and balance (which is to say, humility) in our relations with ourselves, with our fellows, and with God. (*AA Grapevine*, January 1958)

Like Bill, I desire to develop real maturity and balance. I also want to relate better with others, but I have always thought that it may be out of my reach. I had more problems than just alcohol. I'm sober, but what can be done about my problems with living?

I have suffered from clinical depression most of my adult life. I would hear people say at meetings that the same Power that lifted my alcoholism could also cure me of all my other afflictions, including my depression. They said that if I wasn't cured, I needed to go back to the beginning and redo the steps with a more honest intention. I took their suggestion to heart, but as hard as I worked, the depression was not lifted. Why couldn't the program that removed my obsession to drink work on my depression problem? Bill Wilson must have been thinking along the same lines when he wrote a letter to his friend who also shared his affliction of clinical depression.

I kept asking myself, "Why can't the Twelve Steps work to release depression?" By the hour, I stared at the St. Francis prayer … "It is better to comfort than to be comforted." Here was the formula, all right, but why didn't it work?

Suddenly I realized what the matter was … My basic flaw had always been dependence, almost absolute dependence on people or circumstances to supply me with prestige, security, and the like. Failing to get these things according to my perfectionist dreams and specifications, I had fought for them. And when defeat came so did my depression. (*AA Grapevine*, January 1958)

Early on in sobriety I heard someone say, "If you want to get sober, don't drink and go to AA meetings, but if you want what I have, you'll have to turn your life around 180 degrees!" I had just moved to California with about two and a half years of sobriety when this gentleman made that proclamation. I copped an immediate resentment. Who was he to suggest anything about my sobriety? I had almost two and a half years of sobriety! The alcoholic who made the statement had about twenty years sobriety, and I now know he was also more emotionally mature. That was over thirty-three years ago, and I now realize that if I want what he had, my AA efforts will require something more than what I had done.

I heard early on in AA that alcoholics suffer from an affliction with characteristics that can be described by the acronym COG. *They are childish, overly sensitive, and grandiose.* When I first read this description, I thought that it was a bit unfair. Certainly, these rather uncomplimentary adjectives did not apply to all alcoholics, and they did not apply to me. After thousands of meetings and a lot of spiritual work, I have discovered that they not only apply to most alcoholics, but they also apply to me. If I am to grow beyond my arrested state of development, I need to grow up, toughen up, and seek humility. I have heard these admonitions all my life, starting with my parents and throughout my life with coworkers and loved ones. And while I have made baby steps toward these ideals, there is room for growth. My first book chronicled the steps I took to address my addictions and attain a "spiritual awakening." This book will pick up where the first one left off. It will explore what is necessary for me to finally grow up and become emotionally mature.

Additionally, I desire to get along better with others and to play the role that God intends for me each day. As the title of this book suggests, I desire to "live and let live." Just what does it mean to live and let live? To me, it means accepting others who are different from me. It means that I will be tolerant and open-minded without sacrificing my core values.

Sounds simple enough, right? As Bill Wilson discovered, it is a noble goal but not often achieved by those who seek it. It is difficult enough for normal people let alone for alcoholics, even those who have lost the compulsion to drink.

To reach this goal, I have decided to explore beyond what I have done and learned to date. First, I must confirm what it means for me to "live." I can't relate with anyone without a secure knowledge and confidence of what and who I really am. Second, I desire to learn what others suggest on how to better love and tolerate others and live peacefully and usefully in their midst.

The following pages are offered as my contribution to anyone who seeks emotional maturity and relational integrity and, once achieved, to finally be able to live and let live.

1

Emotional Sobriety

Bill Wilson discussed the need for alcoholics to achieve what he called emotional sobriety. He had been sober for over fifteen years and still concluded that there was more to do. After thirty-six years of sobriety, I often feel the same way. I still go to five to nine meetings a week. I help other alcoholics with their journeys through the steps. I start my day with prayer and meditation and end my day reviewing where I may have fallen short. And while my own battle with depression has been mitigated, I still fall victim to its dark grasp. I desire to do more in my recovery. I am eager to pursue the suggestions Bill Wilson left for us. Like Bill, I have considerable time in the program, but I still lack the serenity and peace that many others enjoy. Here is what Bill wrote on the subject.

The Next Frontier: Emotional Sobriety

I think that many oldsters who have put our AA "booze cure" to severe but successful tests still find they often lack emotional sobriety. Perhaps they will be the spearhead for the next major development in AA—the development of much more real maturity and balance (which is to say, humility) in our relations with ourselves, with our fellows, and with God.

Those adolescent urges that so many of us have for top approval, perfect security, and perfect romance—urges quite appropriate to age seventeen—prove to be an impossible way of life when we are at age forty-seven or fifty-seven.

Since AA began, I've taken immense wallops in all these areas because of my failure to grow up, emotionally and spiritually. My God, how painful it is to keep demanding the impossible, and how very painful to discover finally, that all along we have had the cart before the horse! Then comes the final agony of seeing how awfully wrong we have been, but still finding ourselves unable to get off the emotional merry-go-round.

How to translate a right mental conviction into a right emotional result, and so into easy, happy, and good living— well, that's not only the neurotic's problem, it's the problem of life itself for all of us who have got to the point of real willingness to hew to right principles in all our affairs.

Even then, as we hew away, peace and joy may still elude us. That's the place so many of us AA oldsters have come to. And it's a hades of a spot, literally. How shall our unconscious—from which so many of our fears, compulsions and phony aspirations still stream—be brought into line with what we actually believe, know and want! How to convince our dumb, raging and hidden "Mr. Hyde" becomes our main task.

I've recently come to believe that this can be achieved. I believe so because I begin to see many benighted ones—folks like you and me—commencing to get results. Last autumn [several years back—ed.] depression, having no really rational cause at all, almost took me to the cleaners. I began to be scared that I was in for another long chronic spell. Considering the grief I've had with depressions, it wasn't a bright prospect.

I kept asking myself, "Why can't the Twelve Steps work to release depression?" By the hour, I stared at the St. Francis Prayer ... "It's better to comfort than to be the comforted." Here was the formula, all right. But why didn't it work?

Suddenly I realized what the matter was. My basic flaw had always been dependence—almost absolute dependence—on people or circumstances to supply me with prestige, security, and the like. Failing to get these things according to my perfectionist dreams and specifications, I had fought for them. And when defeat came, so did my depression.

There wasn't a chance of making the outgoing love of St. Francis a workable and joyous way of life until these fatal and almost absolute dependencies were cut away.

Because I had over the years undergone a little spiritual development, the absolute quality of these frightful dependencies had never before been so starkly revealed. Reinforced by what Grace I could secure in prayer, I found I had to exert every ounce of will and action to cut off these faulty emotional dependencies upon people, upon AA, indeed, upon any set of circumstances whatsoever.

Then only could I be free to love as Francis had. Emotional and instinctual satisfactions, I saw, were really the extra dividends of having love, offering love, and expressing a love appropriate to each relation of life.

Plainly, I could not avail myself of God's love until I was able to offer it back to Him by loving others as He would have me. And I couldn't possibly do that so long as I was victimized by false dependencies.

For my dependency meant demand—a demand for the possession and control of the people and the conditions surrounding me.

While those words "absolute demand" may look like a gimmick, they were the ones that helped to trigger my release into my present degree of stability and quietness of mind, qualities which I am now trying to consolidate by offering love to others regardless of the return to me.

This seems to be the primary healing circuit: an outgoing love of God's creation and His people, by means of which we avail ourselves of His love for us. It is most clear that the current can't flow until our paralyzing dependencies are broken and broken at depth. Only then can we possibly have a glimmer of what adult love really is.

Spiritual calculus, you say? Not a bit of it. Watch any AA of six months working with a new Twelfth Step case. If the case says, "To the devil with you," the Twelfth Stepper only smiles and turns to another case. He doesn't feel frustrated or rejected. If his next case responds, and in turn starts to give love and attention to other alcoholics, yet gives none back to him, the sponsor is happy about it anyway. He still doesn't feel rejected; instead he rejoices that his one-time prospect is sober and happy. And if his next following case turns out in later time to be his best friend (or romance) then the sponsor is most joyful. But he well knows that his happiness is a by-product—the extra dividend of giving without any demand for a return.

The really stabilizing thing for him was having and offering love to that strange drunk on his doorstep. That was Francis at work, powerful and practical, minus dependency and minus demand.

In the first six months of my own sobriety, I worked hard with many alcoholics. Not a one responded. Yet this work kept me sober. It wasn't a question of those alcoholics giving me anything. My stability came out of trying to give, not out of demanding that I receive.

Thus, I think it can work out with emotional sobriety. If we examine every disturbance we have, great or small, we will find at the root of it some unhealthy dependency and its consequent unhealthy demand. Let us, with God's help, continually surrender these hobbling demands. Then we can be set free to live and love; we may then be able to Twelfth Step ourselves and others into emotional sobriety.

Of course, I haven't offered you a really new idea—only a gimmick that has started to unhook several of my own "hexes" at depth. Nowadays my brain no longer races compulsively in either elation, grandiosity or depression. I have been given a quiet place in bright sunshine. (*AA Grapevine*, January 1958)

As Bill notes, St. Francis had the answer in his prayer. If I can bolster my spiritual condition to meet his suggestions, I will be closer to the goal I seek. This is my prayer today and every day.

Lord, make me an instrument of your peace.
Where there is hatred, let me bring love.
Where there is offense, let me bring pardon.

Where there is discord, let me bring union.
Where there is error, let me bring truth.
Where there is doubt, let me bring faith.
Where there is despair, let me bring hope.
Where there is darkness, let me bring your light.
Where there is sadness, let me bring joy.
O Master, let me not seek as much
to be consoled as to console,
to be understood as to understand,
to be loved as to love,
for it is in giving that one receives,
it is in self-forgetting that one finds,
it is in pardoning that one is pardoned,
it is in dying that one is raised to eternal life. (St. Francis)

During a recent AA meeting, I heard someone share, "If you are doing God's will, you will be happy. Well, you are doing God's will (by staying sober), so be happy!" Applying that premise to what St. Francis suggests, if I practice the tenets of the prayer, I will be doing God's will. If I'm doing God's will, I will be happy. The prayer suggests that I will have to think and behave better particularly in my relationships with other people. And while the AA fellowship and literature have given me everything I know about securing a better relationship not only with God but also with my fellows, I am searching for additional solutions. After all, in "A Vision for You," Bill says, "We realize we know only a little. God will constantly disclose more to you and to us."

I seek to uncover more of what God will reveal to me in my pursuit to achieve emotional sobriety. I will add to what I have already learned and hopefully discover new things to ponder and practice. I am seeking to identify and share solutions I learn from other spirituality seekers. I desire to apply what I learn on how to better relate with others and hope to enjoy better relationships.

I wanted to find out what other alcoholics with significant sober time might think about Bill's letter "The Next Frontier: Emotional Sobriety," so I reached out to several friends in AA for their reactions. Their names have been excluded to respect their anonymity.

Responses to Bill Wilson's Letter
on Emotional Sobriety

Living with the Worst

I enjoyed reading Bill Wilson's letter. I think it's very interesting that what we all need to do is to change our subconscious minds. Our subconscious minds have some primitive, basic ideas that are hard to overcome. When I surrendered way back in 1990, looking back on it, I did it without any proof. In other words, I had to have the faith first. But faith was not enough. I needed to act on that faith, and it was only when I took that leap of faith that my experience changed. I had a powerful spiritual experience.

Regarding Bill's letter, I think that's what happened to Bill. I think it's what happened to a guy that I met today at a meeting. He said he was pushed to a point where he prayed, "God, either save me or kill me; I'm done." And he had a spiritual awakening. I think this is the crux of what we can do that helps change our unconscious minds. What Bill is suggesting can't happen by just thinking about it; we must face that fear and let go willingly. Just like faith. Once we do without absolutely being sure of the outcome, the outcome seems to change.

We have all heard about Pavlov's dogs. What most people don't know is that Pavlov had his laboratory near a riverbank. There was a time when the riverbank flooded at night. His dogs were all left in cages, and as the water seeped in, they began to panic. Fight or flight were their only options, and they could neither fight nor flee. When Pavlov checked on them the next day, he found that the water had gone down. But what really surprised him was that after the dogs were saved, they wouldn't leave the cage. Even though there was no danger. He had to open those cages and forcefully pull those dogs out a few times before they would willingly come out. I think this is a good example of how we let go of our fears. Somehow, we have to be forced to face them.

It's not about hoping for the best. It's more about being willing to face the worst. We decide we can no longer live with the status quo any longer. That's what happened to me. I decided that I would rather live with the worst than live with the status quo.

The Saving Grace of Humility

I've read Bill's treatise on emotional sobriety previously, and from that time forward, I have recognized the critical importance of it for my life. By God's grace, and because of the Twelve Steps and fellowship of Alcoholics Anonymous, the daily compulsion to drink left me many years ago. When people told me at my very first meeting that I was powerless over alcohol and that alcohol was my problem, I connected with that idea and knew I was home. AA folks invited me to keep coming back, and I did—reluctantly at first and then, like a true alcoholic, obsessively. If you had told me at the first meeting that I was also and would continue to be powerless over other people, places, and things, I think I would have been scared off and not returned to AA. If that had happened, I would be dead now.

Along the way, the power of God has relieved me of the obsession to drink. The program told me that I also had to participate in this process if I truly wanted to be free and that the work would continue for my lifetime. I began to believe that and to practice this work to the best of my ability most of the time. When I did slack off, I didn't feel right or good about myself. When life's tragedies tried to take me down, I began ever more so to understand the unconditional and never-ending love and power of God in my life. Even tragedy did not bring on the escapist compulsion to drink. I was and continue to be amazed by this. I began to understand what the expression "life on life's terms" truly means. That does not mean I like it.

God has not only granted me release from the bondage of alcohol but also helped me through all manner of heartbreak and fear without the need to drink. OK, that's done; check the box on the drink obsession. What's next? We say that AA is not so much about the alcohol problem as it is a way of living. I have identified and been working on my character defects for a long, long time. God is helping me. Why then do I still react first much of the time with fear, anger, resentment, selfishness, and/or self-pity when the inevitable "life on life's terms" events occur in my daily living? The self-centeredness that these behaviors stem from is deeply rooted. These behaviors are defense mechanisms. I do not always exhibit such behavior, but I am still undone and frustrated that they exist—until I put myself in God's shoes. He has much more experience than I do in dealing with the spiritual change that brings about recovery from self. As with St. Francis, and with Bill and Bob and countless others, I am a work in progress. I am trying to understand the saving grace of humility and the pathway to inner peace. I am extremely grateful that today I can see these thoughts or behaviors in me even if it is after I already let them out of the cage. Just the fact of recognizing them and the willingness to ask God to help me overcome them is a miraculous part of the AA experience.

Thank God for AA and for Bill's willingness to share his struggle of emotional sobriety. When I first heard the term *emotional sobriety*, I knew exactly what Bill was referring to. He gave it a name, thank God, and he gave us a reminder of the pathway to get there. I do believe this is the essence of our tenth-, eleventh-, and twelfth-step work. And thank God Bill reminds us that it really is our own responsibility to keep doing the work.

Love and Serve

I so identify with Bill and the "adolescent urges" that still trip me up at the age of seventy-five, with thirty-five years of sobriety under my belt. There aren't many years left to enjoy a life of emotional sobriety! I believe in Bill's solution: ridding myself of dependencies on people and circumstances. I have been practicing this the best I know how, and when I do, life is sweet. I can allow people to be who they are, love them as they are, and accept circumstances as being exactly as they are meant to be.

But just as quickly as the flick of a light switch, I can return to that miserable martyr and discontented wretch, "unable to get off the emotional merry-go-round."

So Bill's solution is rightly aligned with God's command for us to love and serve one another, not expecting anything in return. That kind of giving is where peace and joy are found. I have it sporadically; I still have some growing up to do.

Living by the Guidance of God

My life today is directly dependent upon my relationship with God. The phrase "We have a daily reprieve contingent on the maintenance of our spiritual condition" rings true to my heart. The closer I am to my Higher Power each day, the more peace and serenity flow through me. I am loving, tolerant, willing to be of service, and happy. There are also days where I am not so spiritual. In these times, I have come to recognize I am thinking of myself and how things must go my way. In these times, the recognition of God working in my life is overshadowed by my selfishness.

The more I seek God, the more He reveals. The more time I spend with God, the more I understand Him. If I concentrate more on God's will for me instead of my own will, I am able to accept life on life's terms. "Nothing happens in God's world by mistake" is something I repeat to myself throughout the day. This brings me peace and calmness, and I can show love to others.

My greatest thoughts, actions, and plans landed me in the position I was in before Alcoholics Anonymous. Why not try living by the guidance of God? This is a question for which I have no answer accept to comply. My disease of alcoholism is cunning, baffling, and powerful. I must never lose sight that I am completely powerless over alcohol and everything else in my life, and if I am to remain sober and live life to the fullest, I will need God's help.

Staying Active in Sobriety

I realized I was looking at emotional sobriety as not being too happy or too sad.

I was unhappy that I had to stop drinking, but I was so happy there was a solution. But my true nature is one of positivity and cheerfulness, and I'm not anywhere on the "Debbie Downer" spectrum.

In my mind, I drew a little continuum. On one extreme there were extremely manic, happy, and cheerful—even if fake. On the other side was extreme negativity even to the point of ending life. I'll just call it suicide.

I found that I was not somewhere in the middle. I was always on the positive side of the middle.

Now I'm not bipolar, and I have not been diagnosed as bipolar, but I've always gotten excited and worn people out when I go into a project. I'm so full-bore about it, and it pushes people away sometimes if they do not have the same interests. But I've never been on the "down" side.

I don't identify with the part of this article that refers to Bill Wilson and his depression. But I do identify with emotional sobriety. And my emotional sobriety goal was trying to get to even keel, not up from the depths of depression or despair.

I realized that I had medicated myself for years with alcohol to be more like other people, not just the drinking but to be more mellow or laid-back. As I was always working on a project, practicing, and performing music, I was always doing something. And when I wasn't doing something, I was unhappy.

Part of my emotional sobriety is being busy, being physically active, although that's coming to an end as Father Time is catching up with me. But I'm still trying to be as active as I can. I like to be busy, and I like to have projects. And I realize I was moving more to the "manic thing" in the last two weeks because that is the only thing I know how to power. I rationalize I do not have a husband, partner, or family in the area, so I entertain myself. I don't want to say I'm without friends as I have my fellowship in AA, which is very important to me, but I only see them for an hour a day, which like real family is just enough.

But last week, I was moving into projects that were ridiculous and a waste of time. I was enjoying them because I love putting things together and I like taking things apart. I once took my whole dryer apart. Last week I purchased a Christmas tree and for various reasons returned it more than once. Each time I put it together and repackaged it perfectly to return it. The company wanted to hire me because it was so precise. Each package was returned in perfect resalable condition. Was all that necessary?

I discovered that this time spent with some of these projects can be a waste of time. Sometimes I talk about this at the table where there are some kindred spirits who get it and do the same thing.

I am somewhere on the happiness side of the continuum. I went for a run this morning in the snow, and it was freezing and cold. I dressed appropriately and went for a three-mile run. I loved it. I felt so healthy and so happy.

Improving My Outlook

"The Next Frontier" tells a long tale about emotional sobriety, taking Bill W. back to the beginning of AA. I didn't realize that at first, and things felt out of place. I needed to reread it several times before the ideas sunk in correctly—something which happens to me often with AA literature, not to mention AA practices.

So this is really the whole of AA experience and life in this article: how do I improve my outlook and life using AA principles? When I had a few years sobriety under my belt, I often felt I had things together, only to lose it within minutes driving in metro Detroit traffic. I was often shocked at how swiftly I could flip to another person entirely and feel that familiar tension in the pit of my stomach.

But was this really another person, or was this my normal, pre-AA person? My nature has always been selfish; my goal was to see my will done. This may be what I think Bill means by "demands." My only hope for emotional sobriety is to somehow suppress my selfish will, and I think the only way to do that is to seek God's will instead. This has become part of my daily prayers and devotions, and the more I practice, the better I get.

Learning to Love Myself

I am very fortunate. I was born with a silver spoon in my mouth, and it has never been taken away, although I haven't always been aware of it.

Although for my first forty-five to fifty years of life I was riddled with anxiety, a terrible self-image (useless, worthless, incompetent, unlovable) and introversion, these defects were not, for the most part, debilitating. I did not love but was unaware of it. "Thou shalt love thy neighbor as thyself." I did not love myself so I could not love my Higher Power or my neighbor (you).

With sobriety and the many, many people at tables who shared their insecurities with me, I began to see I was neither unique nor alone and began to see myself in a different light. My anxieties began to fade, and my self-image began to improve. I began to see that my Higher Power was doing for me what I could not do for myself. I no longer saw myself as unlovable! I began to love myself. (AA loved me until I learned to love myself.)

I learned that what I resisted persisted and that my life was unmanageable, always had been, and always would be. I needed to leave the management up to my Higher Power.

The ninth step promises began to come true. "Fear of financial insecurity" left me. I learned to love my neighbors as myself. Self-consciousness became greatly reduced. I began to recognize that my Higher Power was doing for me what I could not do for myself. I began to realize that I had what I wanted and wanted what I had. A level of serenity and security descended upon me.

Was it always there? No, but it was usually there and became the norm. What a blessing!

Although I struggled, I was never depressed, so I can't really identify with Bill's letter. I learned that when I got into myself and started feeling sorry for myself, I needed to help someone else.

Early in the program, I found at tables that no matter how bad I was feeling or how hard I felt like I had it at that moment, there was someone who had it worse at that table. Ironically, on the back of one of the pamphlets, I found on the table there was an article entitled "Do Not Judge."

Unhooking from Others

I believe that the observations that Bill makes in the letter are profound. What he advances in the letter certainly applies to me and to others I have met in the recovery community.

To provide my perspective on Bill's letter, I would like to focus on what I believe is Bill's definition of "Emotional Inebriation" that is provided in the beginning of the letter. According to Bill, "My basic flaw had always been dependence—almost absolute dependence—on people or circumstances to supply me with prestige, security, and the like."

In his closing remarks, Bill goes on to say that he has started to unhook himself from the unhealthy dependencies and perfectionist demands that he places on others and that this has helped him with both grandiosity and depression. However, he acknowledges that he feels that he is not offering any new ideas—just the gimmick of "unhooking" from others for their validation as a means of addressing the situation.

Drawing from modern psychology, Buddhism, and through my discussions at the AA tables, I have come to understand that the reason people turn to others for their "prestige, security, and the like" and place "perfectionist demands" on others is low personal self-esteem/self-worth. Without a solid base of self-worth, you will continue to turn to others for validation. As suggested by Bill, a great starting point is to "unhook" yourself from others as a source of your well-being. However, you must take the next steps of understanding what you need to do to improve your intrinsic self-worth.

Emotional Maturity

I believe the title "Emotional Sobriety" is a misnomer. I believe the explanation Bill W. writes about is simply "Emotional Maturity." Bill even states that he had taken many immense wallops because of his failure to grow up emotionally and spiritually.

I personally know that immaturity from experience. I was selfish and self-centered to the core. Just as a child sees the world revolving around himself, I was the same as a man in his late forties. In the process of practicing the Twelve Steps, I found asking my Higher Power to give me the strength and courage to remove my character flaws and to practice the opposite of those character defects and to be charitable and loving. The tenth step also has me checking myself on these defects and living the program's love and tolerance of others daily.

Emotional Sobriety Goals

These generous contributors offered their insights into what they thought emotional sobriety should include. For me, emotional sobriety, when achieved, will permit me to react sanely and normally regardless of the circumstances. It's not about doing away with emotions but accepting them for what they are without going overboard in how I react to them. My behavior will not be driven by my emotions but will reflect a balance between how I feel and how I think. I will be able to respond to life situations maturely and with thoughtful consideration. I will be able to discern between my will and God's will for me. I will be able to relate better with others, accepting them the way they are without sacrificing my true and better self.

Common Themes Suggested by AA

The responses given by those who responded to Bill Wilson's letter on emotional sobriety suggest some common themes.

- growth (rigorous adherence to AA steps ten, eleven, and twelve)
- suppression of selfish will
- conformance to God's will
- acceptance
- love and serve one another
- humility
- positive attitude
- suppression of unhealthy demands upon others
- healthy relationships
- emotional independence
- emotional maturity

2

AA Steps Ten, Eleven, and Twelve

A common response to how AA achieved emotional sobriety includes rigorous and continuous practice of what many AA call the growth steps.

> step ten: continue to take personal inventory and when we are wrong to promptly admitted it
> step eleven: seek through prayer and meditation to improve our conscious contact with God as we understand Him, praying only for knowledge of God's will for us and the power to carry that out
> step twelve: having had a spiritual awakening as the result of these steps, we try to carry this message to alcoholics and practice these principles in all our affairs

Some AA members call these "the maintenance steps," but that suggests they might be staying sober but not growing emotionally or spiritually, sufficient to handle life's severe tests. I must avoid complacency and the possibility of resting on my laurels. I may pay dearly if I let that happen. I want more than just maintenance. I've heard many others in AA share in response to the question "What do I have to change?" They answer the question with *"You have to change everything!"* One good friend in AA shares often at meetings the three things you must do to change:

1. Don't drink.
2. Go to meetings.
3. Do the Twelve Steps.

He says if you do these three things, you will *be* changed. I can attest to that truth. It happened to me. The question for me is what do I do now? I am sober. The obsession to drink has been lifted, so I'm good to go, right? No. Again, if I don't continue to *be* changed, I will likely slip back. Isn't that what a slip really is? For me, it will be going back to the old habits, slipping away from the spiritual solutions, and practicing my defects instead of my program. Just because I have sobriety does not assure me that I will keep it. Steps ten, eleven, and twelve are the price of entry for not only having a spiritual experience but growing my spiritual experience as well.

Daily Examination

Step ten asks me to continue to take a personal inventory and when I am wrong promptly admit it. I know this is crucial to keeping my side of the street clean, but it is also the necessary ingredient to not only maintain relationships with current friends and fellow earthly sojourners but also the basis for establishing new relationships and interactions with others.

> We have entered the world of the Spirit. Our next function is to grow in understanding and effectiveness. This is not an overnight matter. It should continue for our lifetime. Continue to watch for selfishness, dishonesty, resentment, and fear. When these crop up, we ask God at once to remove them. We discuss them with someone immediately and make amends quickly if we have harmed anyone. Then we resolutely turn our thoughts to someone we can help. Love

and tolerance of others is our code. *Alcoholics Anonymous,*
4th ed. (p. 84). AA World Services, Inc.

I look out for my main defects of character. I then ask God to remove them when, *not if,* they crop up. I discuss them with someone immediately—for me it would be my sponsor—and make amends immediately if I have harmed anyone. I turn my thoughts to someone I can help. This means being willing to help anyone, not just an alcoholic. My new code for living leads me to be loving and tolerant.

OK, these are the directions, but where are the specifics on how I should go about these tasks? The Big Book offers the process map, but where are the work instructions? The Big Book calls out my grosser handicaps of selfishness, dishonesty, resentment, and fear. But these are just placeholders for some of my more subtle and maybe even more damaging shortcomings. What about the seven deadly sins: pride, greed, lust, envy, gluttony, wrath, and sloth?

> Practically everybody wishes to be rid of his most glaring and destructive handicaps. No one wants to be so proud that he is scorned as a braggart, nor so greedy that he is labeled a thief. No one wants to be angry enough to murder, lustful enough to rape, gluttonous enough to ruin his health. No one wants to be agonized by the chronic pain of envy or to be paralyzed by sloth. Of course, most human beings don't suffer these defects at these rock-bottom levels. *Twelve Steps and Twelve Traditions* (p. 66). AA World Services, Inc.

What about some of the other stumbling blocks? What about my need to control, my desire to be right, or my intolerance? I believe that if I do not name the *exact nature* of my wrongs, I may overlook them when I ask for God's protection and care as I pray each morning. A mechanical repetition by rote of memorized words may not be thorough enough. As I reflect daily on the major defects of selfishness, dishonesty, resentment, and fear, there may be deeper indiscretions hidden underneath.

When I took my first inventory, I acknowledged my first marriage was not successful. I was young and immature, and I could have listed selfishness and dishonesty as my primary defects of character. But the exact nature of my wrongs needed to be more accurately described. I was a failure as a husband. I did not keep my wedding vows, and I was not a true partner. I did not share parenting responsibilities. I was an absentee dad. I failed to give my son the love and nurturing support he needed during his early childhood. I regret these actions I took during my first marriage. Early on in my disease, I was unable to own my part in my problems. Thank God I am willing and able to change.

The tenth step keeps me honest regarding my part in daily mashups. It might be easy to end my search for my part in my derelictions with by naming the primary defects, but I must also continue to dig deeper to identify the exact nature of my wrongs. I must also continue to validate and own by feelings, but not become a slave to them.

Today I realize I will never have total control, but I desire to learn to better control my responses. I desire to learn to manage my impulses. Like the program suggests, "Without help it is too much for us." I will need to have God's help.

I desire to grow into the spiritual gifts of step ten. Continuing this growth may require a shift in where I am placing my focus. I hear people in the program say they are "working on" their defects that may be keeping them from being as useful as God intends them to be. While I know the intent of what they are saying, they may be missing something. That approach focuses more on the problem and less on the solution. So in addition to "looking out" for my character defects, shouldn't I also be "working on" my character assets?

Defect	Asset
aggressive	gentle
angry	calm
arrogant	humble
boastful	modest
careless	careful
cheating	honest
compulsive	controlled
conceited	modest
critical	tolerant

cynical	open-minded
envying	empathetic
exaggerating	real
fearful	courageous
gossiping	closed mouth
greedy	generous
hateful	loving
inconsiderate	thoughtful
judgmental	tolerant
lustful	pure
rationalizing	honest
resentful	forgiving
rude	polite
sarcastic	sincere
selfish	altruistic
spiteful	forgiving
treacherous	trustworthy
vain	modest
violent	gentle
wasteful	thrifty
willful	yielding

When I am selfish, with God's help, I need to be more generous. When I am defensive, I must be more open to criticism. If the circumstances cause me to become angry, I must try to remain calm. If I exhibit my character assets more than my character defects, won't my relationships improve? If I am willing to practice better behavior, will fewer folks be offended? If my behavior is measured and appropriate for its purpose, I will have done my part. I must not criticize others for their shortcomings but remain focused on being the best version of me.

How can I possibly be of any use to others until I have looked first at my shortcomings? The Bible says that I should not judge others for fear that I will be judged. How can I be of any use to those I would help to stay sober until I have cleaned up my own mess?

What about the seven deadly sins? They are long known to be the scourge of humankind. I addressed my behavior while drinking for each of these sins when I did my first fourth step. I owe a debt to the person who shared his fourth and fifth steps with me before I wrote my inventory. It really made it easier for me to get honest and to look more closely at my part in the harms I caused others. He directed me to the Big Book of Alcoholics Anonymous for guidance, but thankfully he also asked me to add instances where my behavior while drinking may have caused me to commit each of the seven deadly sins.

Since then, I have also discovered items on the other side of the ledger. For each of the seven deadly sins, I found what the church calls the seven virtues. In essence, these virtues are the cure for their corresponding sins. I clearly will benefit from looking daily as to where I am on the continuum between sins and virtues.

Seven Deadly Sins	Continuum	Corresponding Virtue
pride	⟵⟶	humility
greed	⟵⟶	charity
lust	⟵⟶	chastity
anger	⟵⟶	patience
gluttony	⟵⟶	temperance
envy	⟵⟶	kindness
slothfulness	⟵⟶	diligence

Another way to look at these opposites of the behavioral spectrum is to look at the virtues as not just a cure but also a preemptive action. For instance, if I know I am going to be in an interaction that just might lead to anger, particularly if this has been a pattern with individuals or groups, I should concentrate on specific ways that I can demonstrate patience. I don't have to surrender my beliefs or even waver on my position, but I must try to listen and understand the other person's point of view.

This little exercise can help me retrain the way I think and behave which will ultimately lead to improving the way I feel. The only thing I can control is me and my attitudes, so if I want to think more positively, perhaps I should think more about positive outcomes. Migrating this into my inventory work means I will have to look at my movement on the continuum of defects and assets with an eye toward how much I've changed for the better and not just on how many times I've faltered.

Seven Deadly Needs

I read a book by Edward Bear entitled *The Seven Deadly Needs.* This book does a very good job of identifying the problem inherent in each of those needs and then treats implications of each of them then offers solutions in a forthright manner. I believe it dovetails well with AA principles and gives me more to ponder as I think about my daily inventory.

I have added my thoughts and reactions for each of them. I will add these "needs" to my list of things I need to watch for and avoid as I interact with others.

The Need to Know

People have said that knowledge may be power, and there is nothing wrong with being in the know. Education and self-knowledge are critical pieces of individual growth and usefulness. It becomes deadly when it evolves from pride, ego, and selfishness. It is particularly deadly when it emanates from an inability to trust. A lack of trust can ruin relationships. When a partner incessantly queries for another's whereabouts and details of activities, it may be seen being overly controlling. It may reveal unearned suspicion or a lack of trust. If I am to grow spiritually, I need to stop focusing on others' perceived indiscretions and start focusing on my own opportunities for improvement.

I have been accused by one of my sponsees of needing to know the underlying reasons for things. He calls it digging for the "reason behind the reason." This is unproductive in two ways. First, I may be jumping to conclusions about the motives for others' actions. Second, I should leave the autopsy of people's behavior to those more qualified to diagnose. Amateur psychology leads to damaged relationships.

The Need to Be Right

If I come across as always being right, I will eventually drive others away. No one likes a know-it-all. Relational maturity requires a willingness to consider individual points of view and experiences. The "all right" or "all wrong" approach in relationships leads to predictable conflict with those who think and behave differently from me.

The truth is I am often wrong. Doubling down on my position even after the facts have been revealed can ruin credibility and—even worse—destroy friendships. This might be seen as immaturity and perhaps a need to compensate for insecurity. If it isn't quelled, it can lead to unnecessary arguments and escalation of conflict.

The Need to Get Even

I have heard coworkers say something like "I may forgive, but I will never forget." This desire to get even likely grows from deeper defects of character like pride, selfishness, and fear. My pride says, "How dare you?" My fear says, "You have taken something, and I want it back."

For me, there is no room for revenge or any overt or covert effort to even the score. Alcoholics Anonymous says that resentment is the number one offender. Jesus suggests we should turn the other cheek. A tit for tat attitude will not give me peace of mind. Even if others have wronged me, the sources I trust say that forgiveness is the answer.

The Need to Look Good

A coworker once told me that I should blow my own horn. He suggested that if I didn't, "others will use it as a spittoon." If I didn't promote my accomplishments, others would ignore them or—even worse—see me as nonthreatening.

The issue really comes down to "Who I am working for?" In the dog-eat-dog work world, I had to be on guard. I was always watching my back for those who might be competing unfairly. I desire to grow spiritually, so today God is my employer today. I know that God is love. Seeking

God's love does not require anything other than being OK with who I am becoming with His help. I hear often at the AA tables, "What anyone thinks of me is none of my business." Falling back to the temptations of the world doesn't work. Will I need the worldly trimmings of success to attract God? Never. He loves me and desires an authentic relationship. I must give up on the idea that the world will ever care about what I achieve or accomplish.

The size of my home, the status of my car, the quality of my clothing, or my trips to exotic places were never enough to impress the world. Sadly, I can still be pulled away to seek the false promise these material things fail to deliver. Selfishness, pride, ego, and greed conspire to lead me to taking another dip in the temptation pool. Holy Spirit, save me from temptation.

The Need to Judge

The Bible suggests if I judge, I will be judged. I think this need relates closely to the need to be right. I may be quick to jump to a solution for others that may not be appropriate for them or consistent with God's will for them. Most often these judgments are fueled by my preconceived notions, which may or may not be correct. I had better stick to taking my own inventory rather than taking another's. I have heard people share at meetings that I should judge myself critically and judge others with empathy and compassion. I need to be hard on me and easy on others.

There is a section of the Big Book often read at AA meetings called "Acceptance." It is an often a mainstay of items read before meetings. The paragraph that follows that section, while not read as often, cautions of the dangers of judging others.

> Shakespeare said, "All the world's a stage, and all the men and women merely players." He forgot to mention that I was the chief critic. I was always able to see the flaw in every person, every situation. And I was always glad to point it out, because I knew you wanted perfection, just as I did. AA and acceptance have taught me that there is a bit of good in the worst of us and a bit of bad in the best of us; that we are all

children of God and we each have a right to be here. When
I complain about me or about you, I am complaining about
God's handiwork. I am saying that I know better than God.
*Inc, AA World Services. Alcoholics Anonymous, 4ᵗʰ ed. (p.
417). AA World Services, Inc.*

What would cause me to judge others prematurely or without merit?
I may be trying to build myself up by tearing someone else down. I may
be intolerant and closed-minded. Who am I to think I know all the
facts that may be contributing to anyone's behavior? The antidote for
my misplaced need to judge requires me to be more tolerant and open-
minded. I often cry for justice when I should be praying for mercy. I
desire to be more tolerant and less judgmental.

The Need to Keep Score

This deadly need keeps me focused on myself, and selfishness is one of
my most dangerous defects of character. It is related closely to getting
even. I have a shopping addiction. My wife and I sometimes play a costly
game. If she buys something, then I must buy something of equal or
greater value to even the score.

I am competitive, and the indication of whether I win or lose is
determined by "keeping score." If my self-worth is so fragile that I can't
be a good loser or I am unable to accept another's good fortune without
feeling less than or deprived, I am likely not growing toward emotional
maturity.

The Need to Control

One of the most common words I hear during AA meetings is the word
control. The Big Book says this about control:

> We alcoholics are men and women who have lost the ability
> to control our drinking. We know that no real alcoholic ever
> recovers control. All of us felt at times that we were regaining
> control, but such intervals—usually brief—were inevitably

followed by still less control, which led in time to pitiful and incomprehensible demoralization.

Inc, AA World Services. *Alcoholics Anonymous,* 4th ed. (p. 30). AA World Services, Inc.

I cannot control my drinking, and I cannot control my surroundings. I am powerless over people, places, and things. The Big Book tells the story of an actor who is trying to control the play. The other actor doesn't know his lines and the sets and lighting are not being managed to his expectation. He tries at first to be nice with others as he communicates his desire, but they do not respond. He becomes more demanding. He is no longer so nice. He raises his voice, shouting his demands. He steps on their toes, and they retaliate. Attempts to control other people do not work. I must watch closely to avoid this deadly need. Instead, I will move toward letting go of my expectations of others. This is my cue to "let go and let God."

Spiritual Connection: Prayer and Meditation

I am growing daily in my faith, but I desire an even greater personal connection with my Savior Jesus Christ. I truly want Jesus to have all of me.

If I pray and meditate, I will have a conscious contact with my Higher Power. I pray for knowledge of God's will for me and the power to carry that out. I ask God to direct my thinking, but I need to remember to ask that my thinking should be divorced from self-pity, dishonest or self-seeking motives.

I ponder the notion that if I do God's will, I will be happy. That leads to the conclusion that if I remain sober, I will be doing God's will, so I should therefore be happy! I wonder though is "being happy" enough. I can have the kind of happiness suggested by the expression "fat, dumb, and happy." I believe that being happy is not as important as being useful. I do seek a conscious contact with Jesus, and I desire to share whatever I have left of my journey in this realm by achieving a secure, sincere personal relationship with Him.

There's an old hymn I used to sing as a child growing up in the

Baptist church that describes my intention. I can't remember all the verses, but the chorus went something like "Just a closer walk with Thee. Grant it, Jesus, is my plea."

I want to know my Higher Power, Jesus, better. I have been told that belief in Christ will change me. I will not only be changed for the better, but I will be changed in all the ways God desires for me to be of maximum service for His ends to be met. This goes well beyond mere happiness; this goes all the way to joy! I will be happy, joyous, free, sober, useful, and at peace knowing I am doing God's will. Are there additional gifts? St. Paul suggests I will know the fruits of the Spirit.

> But the fruit of the Spirit is love, joy, peace, forbearance, kindness, goodness, faithfulness, gentleness and self-control. Against such things there is no law. (Galatians 5:22–23 NIV)

Instead of praying for specific outcomes, I will just focus on connecting with the Holy Spirit. The Spirit is the source for everything I desire. I believe there are more gifts possible by a consistent practice of establishing a conscious contact through sustained prayer and meditation. I'm discovering that more can be achieved based on how I meditate and pray. I am finally learning that the real gift of prayer and meditation is not just establishing conscious contact. It is praying for the knowledge and power to do God's will. Come, Holy Spirit. Come.

In my first book, I talked about atonement—or as I refer to it, at-one-ment. I devoted an entire chapter to the topic. As a reminder, here are the *Merriam-Webster's Collegiate Dictionary* definitions for the word *atonement*.

> 1: reparation for an offense or injury: He wanted to find a way to make atonement for his sins.
> 2: the reconciliation of God and humankind through the sacrificial death of Jesus Christ
> 3: Christian Science: the exemplifying of human oneness with God (*Merriam-Webster's Collegiate Dictionary*)

Definitions 2 and 3 are the ones that I now believe contain the answer for my recovery from all my addictions.

I want to be totally in sync with God's will for me. I must admit to my own shortcomings and ignorance of the signs that God provides. I may not always get a clear-cut direction of what God wants from me. One of my sponsees tells me of a time when he too was uncertain of what God's will for him might be. He said that he was about to do his daily reading and meditations and what happened next was somewhat miraculous. Without looking specifically for any passage, he randomly opened his Bible and was surprised to find the following verse:

> Rejoice always,
> pray continually,
> give thanks in all circumstances; for this is God's will for you
> in Christ Jesus. (1 Thessalonians 5:16–18 NIV)

What a revelation! Now when I am in doubt about God's will for me, I have this verse. There are times still when I feel like there is more to be accomplished in the execution of God's will for me. This is when I need to be on guard.

> We alcoholics are undisciplined. So we let God discipline us
> in the simple way we have just outlined.
>   AA World Services. *Alcoholics Anonymous,* 4th ed. (p. 88). AA World Services, Inc.

The Bible also points out that I need to be watchful. I do need to maintain a conscious contact, but I can't rest on my laurels thinking that I'm off the hook because I have prayed and meditated. In addition to my conscious contact, I need to be *consciously aware* of my shortcomings, or if you will, my sins. I need to let the steps and the scripture guide and correct my thoughts and actions.

> All Scripture is God-breathed and is useful for teaching, rebuking, correcting and training in righteousness, so that the servant of God may be thoroughly equipped for every good work. (2 Timothy 3:16–17 NIV)

Behaving Better: Helping Others and
Practicing AA Principles

I want daily to "do every good work." This is the final piece of the puzzle. It is the realization of the *spiritual awakening* promised if I complete all the steps of the AA program. If I really enjoy the fruits of the spirit—love, joy, peace, patience, kindness, goodness, faithfulness, gentleness, and self-control—why wouldn't I be compelled to help other alcoholics to find this program and practice these principles in all my affairs? There is a hymn, "Blessed Assurance," I used to sing that speaks to this assurance.

> Blessed assurance, Jesus is mine
> O what a foretaste of glory divine
> Heir of salvation, purchase of God
> I'm born of his Spirit and washed in his blood
> This is my story, this is my song
> Praising my Savior, all the day long
> This is my story, this is my song
> Praising my Savior all the day long ...

The lyrics were written in 1873 by blind hymn writer Fanny Crosby to the music written in 1873 by Phoebe Knapp.

I had a dream the other night that included a discussion with someone about the relationship between AA's third step and the twelfth step from the Big Book of Alcoholics Anonymous.

Step three: "Made a decision to turn our will and life over to the care of God as we understood him."

Step twelve: "Having had a spiritual awakening as the result of these steps, we tried to carry the message to alcoholics and to practice the AA principles in all of our affairs."

I heard myself telling this person in my dream about the progression of what happens when I decided to turn my will and my life over to the care of a Power greater than myself. The other person said that the will represents his thinking, and his life is his actions. I argued that life includes more than a person's actions. I said that the steps treat the three-part disease we have by treating body, mind, and spirit. I said that the first step if practiced perfectly keeps me from ingesting alcohol and that if I do that successfully, my health and body will improve. I added that the third step implicitly adds a commitment to improve my will, or my mind, by doing the remaining steps.

In the dream, I added that the third step does not address the "third part" of our disease: the spirit. That only happens if I do the personal work required in steps four through eleven. Then and only then will I have a "spiritual awakening." This awakening of spirit is what compels me to act "spiritually different" by helping others and practicing spiritual principles.

What a revelation. It's true! I will begin to give away what was so freely given. My attitude toward life and others will change away from a material perspective to one that is spiritual. Chuck C said that it was like he was given a new pair of glasses. In essence, I will begin to see what I couldn't see before. Perhaps this spiritual perspective was always there and I was just too blinded by the trappings of the world to see it. On the other hand, perhaps I do not have to give up "all" of my old ideas completely but reframe them in the context of seeing them from an emotionally sober perspective.

It may not be the education that comes from an intense dive into sophisticated concepts and philosophies, but perhaps it was from the ability to finally see what was always there. We were finally awakened to see the truth about ourselves. Or conversely, because we were finally able to see the truth about ourselves, we were awakened. We were finally able to accept and celebrate the persons that God intended us to be. *Alcoholics Anonymous Twelve Steps and Twelve Traditions* describes it this way:

> When a man or a woman has a spiritual awakening, the most important meaning of it is that he has now become able to do, feel, and believe that which he could not do before on his unaided strength and resources alone. He has been granted a gift which amounts to a new state of consciousness and being. He has been set on a path which tells him he is really going somewhere, that life is not a dead end, not something to be endured or mastered. In a very real sense he has been transformed, because he has laid hold of a source

of strength which, in one way or another, he had hitherto denied himself. He finds himself in possession of a degree of honesty, tolerance, unselfishness, peace of mind, and love of which he had thought himself quite incapable. What he has received is a free gift, and yet usually, at least in some small part, he has made himself ready to receive it.

This is nothing short of miraculous! What is even more miraculous is that the miracle happened to me. It took a lot of effort and a lot of faith to go from a questioning doubter unsure of whether I really was an addict to being transformed and renewed through a spiritual experience. But I can't take credit for the miracle. I give God the credit. I will be forever grateful. I did receive numerous gifts as the *Twelve Steps and Twelve Traditions* describes. I do have a source of strength which was promised, but I doubted it until I finally experienced it. The Big Book describes a gold miner who finally hit the motherlode, only to find that the only way he could keep it was to give it all away. This is especially true for the twelfth step. The rubber hits the road when I complete the circle and start acting as though I am spiritually awake by helping other alcoholics to get what I have been so freely given. And the gifts keep coming.

> Life will take on new meaning. To watch people recover, to see them help others, to watch loneliness vanish, to see a fellowship grow up about you, to have a host of friends—this is an experience you must not miss. We know you will not want to miss it. Frequent contact with newcomers and with each other is the bright spot of our lives.
> Inc, AA World Services. *Alcoholics Anonymous*, 4th ed. (p. 89). AA World Services, Inc.,

While this kind of work in AA has its own rewards as suggested in the aforementioned "promises," the work requires patience and understanding beyond what many people are equipped to give. It certainly requires God's help and direction. Keeping my own house in order and continuing to be guided toward God's will for me is prerequisite. After all, I can't give away what I don't have. I believe the work I do to explore the additional tools available to me as I seek emotional sobriety will provide even more impetus to *live and let live*.

3

Common Elements of Emotional Sobriety

Here again are the topics I gleaned from responses provided by my AA friends about emotional sobriety:

- suppression of selfish will
- conformance to God's will
- acceptance
- love and serve one another
- humility
- positive attitude
- suppression of unhealthy demands upon others
- healthy relationships
- emotional independence
- emotional maturity

I am grateful for these responses from my sober friends. I asked only those friends with significant recovery time to participate. Their generous contributions motivated me to add my thoughts and observations for each of these common elements. I am hopeful that our collective considerations will prove useful to all those, like me, who desire to *live and let live.*

Suppressing Self-Will

A lot of my prayers end with "Thy will, not mine, be done." Often, I say this by rote, just a throwaway sentence at the end of a prayer without much sincerity or conviction. When I take the time to focus on my truth, I know that self-will and selfishness are underlying obstacles that keep me from doing God's will and ultimately keep me from being happy, joyous, and free.

> The requirement is that we be convinced that any life run on self-will can hardly be a success. On that basis we are almost always in collision with something or somebody, even though our motives are good. p. 60, *Big Book of Alcoholics Anonymous*

The focus on self keeps me in a self-imposed prison. I think, ponder, and ruminate. I wonder, *What is to be? What will happen to me? Why is this happening to me?* Of course, these thoughts are rarely helpful either to me or to those I would help. The focus on self is a bad habit. The more I think about myself, the more likely I will focus further and further inward. If this is left unchecked, my thoughts become more and more negative, which can lead me to self-criticism and perhaps even to self-destruction. In the past, this pattern of negative self-talk led to isolation. And isolation led to pitiful and incomprehensible demoralization. I drank. The more I drank, the more I hated the dependency on self that led to self-doubt and self-hatred. And once I drank, I was no longer of any use to myself or to others.

> So our troubles, we think, are basically of our own making. They arise out of ourselves, and the alcoholic is an extreme example of self-will run riot, though he usually doesn't think so. Above everything, we alcoholics must be rid of this selfishness. We must, or it kills us!"
> Inc, AA World Services. *Alcoholics Anonymous*, 4th ed. (p. 62). AA World Services, Inc.,

This was a pattern I truly can see in myself. Can selfishness kill? I came close to proving it true.

One night after excessive drinking, I returned home to find everyone in bed. It was a summer night with a warm rain, and it seemed that a good way to sober up a bit would be to take a walk. As I often did when I drank too much, I peeled off all my clothes except for briefs with hearts on them my wife had given me for Valentine's Day. So there I was, walking down a busy street in my underwear, totally oblivious to how that might appear to the passersby. In fact, no one seemed to notice. I know now that I must have had some desire to be rescued. The decision to walk in near nudity was unsuccessful, so I returned totally drenched and still without any consolation or peace. I decided to end it all once and for all. I got my shotgun and sat on the steps that led to the upstairs bedrooms. I would show them. When they awoke, they would be forced to see my lifeless body surrounded with the gore that a shotgun blast can yield. It would be final and dramatic, literally going out with a bang. Still thinking about myself, I decided that the gore-filled ending might be a bit too dramatic.

I struck a compromise. I would consider the feelings of those who would find my disfigured corpse. I would go out on the back-porch stairs to commit the deed. I reasoned that the rain would wash away some of the gore; thus, I was considering the feelings of others. Alcohol, or God, mercifully transitioned me into blackout before I could act on any of my thoughtless choices. During the blackout, I had put the shotgun away, and I awoke the next morning hungover but still alive.

> Selfishness—self-centeredness! That, we think, is the root of our troubles. Driven by a hundred forms of fear, self-delusion, self-seeking, and self-pity, we step on the toes of our fellows and they retaliate. Sometimes they hurt us, seemingly without provocation, but we invariably find that at some time in the past we have made decisions based on self which later placed us in a position to be hurt.
>
> AA World Services. *Alcoholics Anonymous,* 4th ed. (p. 62). AA World Services, Inc.

I've heard folks in AA meetings introduce themselves with something like "I'm an alcoholic, and my problem is (their name)." So the quote from above is correct. I step on the toes of my fellows, and they retaliate. I am the one who was always present during most of my problems. I had a part in most of the issues that caused me to resent, lie, run away, and attack without provocation. I did all of it in the name of self-preservation and self-justification. My favorite pronouns were *I, me, my* and *mine*. This had to change. Today, if my focus is solely on me, I am asking for trouble. Even if I mask this selfishness with false humility, I remain in self. A friend used to say, "I don't think very much of myself, but I am all I think of." Negative self-focus it still is an obsession with self.

I must find a way to become less selfish and self-centered, if I am ever to have even a small measure of serenity. My goal is to rely less on my will and rely more on God's will. The Twelve Steps of Alcoholics Anonymous are permitting me to achieve that goal. I am becoming more spiritually awake as I continue to work the steps. I am transitioning from doing my will to doing God's will.

> God grant me the serenity to accept the things I cannot change, courage to change the things I can, and wisdom to know the difference. Thy will, not mine, be done.
> *Alcoholics Anonymous World Service, Inc. Twelve Steps and Twelve Traditions (p. 41). AA World Services, Inc.*

The first time I recall seeing this prayer was on a plaque located on the wall of my mother-in-law's kitchen. While I was drinking, I saw it numerous times as I was returning to the refrigerator to get another beer. It wasn't until I got sober that I started to appreciate the importance of this simple but profound request. When I glanced at the plaque in subsequent sober visits, I was grateful for all that my new life permitted. Even though I resented them in my early married life, I learned to accept my mother-in-law and her husband in a completely new way. I learned that I could not change them, nor would I ever want to change them. I learned to accept them just the way they were.

I recall becoming physically sick numerous times during trips to visit with my wife's folks. I would rationalize that I had been working too hard and was worn down. The truth was I was in a toxic environment that provided a preview of coming attractions for the progression of my disease. I now know that since I couldn't change the environment, and because I lacked acceptance, I lacked serenity. There is a direct correlation between acceptance and serenity. If I am unwilling or unable to accept things that I cannot change, I cannot have serenity. I have since seen a quote I picked up somewhere along the way that says something like "God may not stop the storm, but He will give you peace during the storm." I was never able to muster anything even close to serenity while drinking.

As my friend who submitted one of the responses to this book said, "We have to be comfortable, or at least be willing, to face the worst." I heard an acronym for the word FEAR: face everything and recover. This could be the root cause of why I am unable to accept life on life's terms, and even more so, when I am trying to muster the courage to make needed changes in myself. Fear is that corrosive thread that permeates my attitudes and paralyzes my ability to act. I recently was at an AA meeting where I shared that my prayers include asking God to relieve me not only from the bondage of self but also from dishonesty, resentment, and fear. My friend shared that the root cause of these and all my shortcomings is fear. I must accept that fear is the likely culprit in all my efforts to accept the things I cannot change, just as it is when I lack the willingness to "change the things I can."

Fear is the opposite of courage. I suspect that fear is one of the devil's favorite weapons. When I need the "courage to change," I must have God's help. The first two words of the Serenity Prayer contain the key: "God grant." Serenity really is a gift, and I must ask God to bestow it to me daily. I need this daily gift to face life on life's terms.

Conformance to God's Will

What is God's will for me? In a general sense, I believe I have a pretty good idea what God's will for me. The question is not so much if I know God's will but whether I will conform to it or not. As a recovering alcoholic, I know God wants me to stay sober and to help other alcoholics to achieve sobriety. I also believe that God wants me to behave in a manner that is pleasing to Him.

Rejoice always,
pray continually,
give thanks in all circumstances; for this is God's will for you
in Christ Jesus. (1 Thessalonians 5:16–18 NIV)

Therefore, I urge you, brothers and sisters, in view of God's
mercy, to offer your bodies as a living sacrifice, holy and
pleasing to God—this is your true and proper worship.

Do not conform to the pattern of this world, but be
transformed by the renewing of your mind. Then you will
be able to test and approve what God's will is—his good,
pleasing and perfect will. (Romans 12:1–2 NIV)

Be very careful, then, how you live—not as unwise but as
wise, making the most of every opportunity, because the days
are evil. Therefore do not be foolish, but understand what
the Lord's will is. Do not get drunk on wine, which leads to
debauchery. Instead, be filled with the Spirit, speaking to one
another with psalms, hymns, and songs from the Spirit. Sing
and make music from your heart to the Lord, always giving
thanks to God the Father for everything, in the name of our
Lord Jesus Christ. (Ephesians 5:15–20 NIV)

Most of my opportunities to do God's will happen when I am
interacting with other people. I interact in person, voice-to-voice,
and via social media, Zoom, and text. Before I interact with others, I
have found that I have greater success if I consider the following three
questions before I speak:

> Is it true?
> Is it kind?
> Is it necessary?

These same three questions should be applied to what I think! Why
would I permit thoughts that aren't true or unkind? Aren't there also
times when I pursue thoughts about things that are unnecessary? Why
wouldn't I be willing to keep my thought life on a higher plane? What
should I think about instead?

Every day is a day when we must carry the vision of God's will into all of our activities. "How can I best serve Thee— Thy will (not mine) be done." These are thoughts which must go with us constantly. We can exercise our will power along this line all we wish. It is the proper use of the will.

Inc, AA World Services. Alcoholics Anonymous, 4th ed. (p. 85). AA World Services, Inc.,

I have a sponsee who clarifies what he thinks a couple of the words mean to him when he discusses the third step. He made a decision to turn his life and will over to the care of God as he understands him. He says that "will" means our thoughts and that "life" means our actions. I don't disagree. How I think will drive my attitudes, and my attitudes will influence how I will behave. A negative attitude leads me to become the victim who looks at the world through selfish and self-centered filters. This perspective becomes the catalyst for fear and resentment, which either drives me to act out in anger or to sink into depressive isolation. I am then no longer useful to God or my fellows.

Conversely a positive attitude leads to positive behavior and ultimately a more useful life. What do I do to assure positivity? I will start each day with prayer and meditation. I will pray for knowledge of God's will for me and the power to carry that out. I will pray that God divorces my thinking from negative thoughts and to guard me from selfishness, dishonesty, resentment, and fear. I will read daily meditations and use an app to listen to daily meditations. If I do this to start my day, I will be more likely to remain on a spiritual path, which will help me to more confident throughout my day. Throughout the day, I will pause when agitated and pray for the next right thing to do. Will I ever be perfect at this? No, but I am completely willing to grow along spiritual lines. I hope then I will be less likely to surrender to worry and despair. I will have more confidence and more energy. I won't tire as easily, and I will be more inclined to do the next right thing.

There is another definition of the word *will* that I heard lately. It can be described as the "eye" of the soul. Early on in sobriety, I heard alcoholism described as "soul sickness." If this is true, and I believe that it is, then I had better be concerned with the condition of my soul. I must choose my will or God's will. I choose to do God's will.

Acceptance

Most of the meetings I attend begin with a moment of silence followed by the Serenity Prayer.

> With each passing day of our lives, may every one of us sense more deeply the inner meaning of AA's simple prayer: God grant us the serenity to accept the things we cannot change, Courage to change the things we can, And wisdom to know the difference.
> *Alcoholics Anonymous World Service, Inc. Twelve Steps and Twelve Traditions (p. 126). AA World Services, Inc.*

The quality of my acceptance boils down to just how well I deal with the things I cannot change. I have learned that acceptance is directly proportional to the amount of serenity I have been granted. As I have already shared, the events in my life drive my attitude. My attitude drives my behavior. On my own, I won't have the serenity I need to cope with the things I cannot change.

Early on during the COVID-19 pandemic, I spent a considerable time in a stay-at-home directive to not leave my home for any other reason than food or medical necessity. To most nonalcoholics, this necessity to stay at home to "flatten the curve" of new cases of COVID-19 made sense. I vacillated between compliance to do my part and rebellion to fight the directive. I find myself rebelling against what many describe as the "new normal." I understood that if I lacked the serenity sufficient to stay the course, I may have been putting myself and others at risk. Alternatively, I felt that there had been significant overreach to the point my rights were being abused. Perhaps I should have filtered my emotional responses with questions like "Is action required? Does it have to be done by me? And does it have to be done now?" I would then have more likely to arrive at a rational conclusion. I would have decided that there was little I could have done other than to accept the things I could not change and to change what I was able to change: me and my attitudes.

The Big Book has one of the stories at the back of the book entitled "And Acceptance Was the Answer." It contains an often read passage heard being read during AA meetings that stresses the power and importance of acceptance as a solution.

> And acceptance is the answer to all my problems today. When I am disturbed, it is because I find some person, place, thing, or situation—some fact of my life—unacceptable to me, and I can find no serenity until I accept that person, place, thing, or situation as being exactly the way it is supposed to be at this moment. **Nothing, absolutely nothing, happens in God's world by mistake.** Until I could accept my alcoholism, I could not stay sober; unless I accept life completely on life's terms, I cannot be happy. I need to concentrate not so much on what needs to be changed in the world as on what needs to be changed in me and in my attitudes.
>
> *Inc, AA World Services. Alcoholics Anonymous, 4th ed. (p. 417). AA World Services, Inc.*

I find it interesting that some in AA have a problem with the sentence displayed in bold italics that says, "Nothing, absolutely nothing, happens in God's world by mistake." In one of the meetings I attend, members conducted a "group conscience" to delete that sentence entirely from the reading. I guess they find it objectionable or perhaps unacceptable. Ironic, isn't it, that some folks find a beloved passage on acceptance unacceptable? There is another passage that follows that is not as well-known but might be just as important to those who need to remember the source of the serenity they seek.

> Shakespeare said, "All the world's a stage, and all the men and women merely players." He forgot to mention that I was the chief critic. I was always able to see the flaw in every person, every situation. And I was always glad to point it out, because I knew you wanted perfection, just as I did. AA and acceptance have taught me that there is a bit of good in the worst of us and a bit of bad in the best of us; that we are all children of God and we each have a right to be here. When I complain about me or about you, I am complaining about God's handiwork. I am saying that I know better than God."
>
> *Inc, AA World Services. Alcoholics Anonymous, 4th ed. (p. 417). AA World Services, Inc.*

This passage reinforces my need to practice love and tolerance in all my affairs. I don't have to like everyone, but I must respect that all are children of God. When I find anyone unacceptable, I am really complaining about God's handiwork. I am in trouble if I take on the role of critic. Unnecessary judgment is a barrier to my spiritual growth. Therefore, I will stop complaining about others and myself. Like my mother used to tell me, God doesn't make junk.

I remember reading in the Big Book of Alcoholics Anonymous that God either is or He isn't. He is everything or He is nothing. It forces me to choose. I believe that God is and that He is everything. He is the source of my serenity, and when I acknowledge Him, He grants me serenity sufficient to accept the things I cannot change. The serenity I need is not earned or conjured. I cannot "will" it. It is granted. My acceptance is contingent on my humility. Without humility, God assumes I do not need his help.

I must accept other people just the way they are, including their choices of a Higher Power. Are these people able to grow spiritually not knowing the God of my understanding? Is it possible that even atheists and agnostics who pray the Serenity Prayer can pray to a power of their own understanding? Is the atheist's god of their understanding capable of granting serenity? Does this "god" of reason, collective consciousness, set of principles, or the like grant serenity? Over the years, I have watched atheists and agnostics practice their program, and I must report that many have become spiritually awake. Serenity seems granted to those who don't believe in my God. Could this awareness be another small step toward my ability to live and let live? Perhaps. My tolerance of others' choices regarding a Higher Power does not affect my personal decision. My choice is to love God and my Savior Jesus Christ with all my heart, with all my soul, and with all my mind and to love all others as I love myself. I guess it really boils down to how long a person wants to live. Atheists and agnostics may enjoy a spiritual awakening sufficient to permit them to die sober. Christian alcoholics like me will not only live a sober life but after the death of the body they will live eternally in heaven.

Love and Serve One Another

Loving myself and others has always been my goal. Almost everyone knows the Bible verse that has been referred to as the "greatest commandment."

> "Teacher, which is the greatest commandment in the Law?"
> Jesus replied: "'Love the Lord your God with all your heart and with all your soul and with all your mind.'
> This is the first and greatest commandment.
> And the second is like it: 'Love your neighbor as yourself.'
> All the Law and the Prophets hang on these two commandments." (Matthew 22:36–40 NIV)

Love is the answer, but only God can love perfectly, so I must be satisfied with a level of love that only a human can achieve. As the verse suggests, if I know God, I will know love. I was recently taken aback with a bumper sticker I saw that said, "My religion is love." My first thought was *What sacrilege!* Upon further reflection, there may have been some justification for the bumper sticker's claim.

> Whoever does not love does not know God, because God is love. (1 John 4:8 NIV)

Emotional sobriety includes the ability to love without any expectation. There are the following four types of love that the Bible sources from the Greek:

- agape: unselfish love
- phileo: brotherly love
- eros: erotic love
- storge: love between family members

It is agape or unselfish love that I desire. Biblical writers used God as the standard for true agape. That would hold me to a standard that I can never achieve, but I do desire to want for others what I want for myself and have general empathy and lovingkindness for all people.

I was brought up in a loving family and can recall the love I felt for my parents and my sisters. As I got older, I was fortunate to be able to connect with friends with whom I shared brotherly love.

Somewhere along the way, I was attracted to friends of the opposite sex with more than a platonic association. I mistakenly rationalized that this was love, and in certain instances, it might have been. If I am honest though, the love I felt in my adolescent years and well into adulthood was far from selfless. I am sure that the spiritual awakening that leads to service requires more of agape or sacrificial love. This is the love that permits me to give without expectation for anything in return.

Before I could experience agape love, I had to accept the unconditional love God has for me. This evolved for me over time. For a long time, I found it difficult to believe that God loved me. I saw myself as full of sin and flaws and therefore I would never measure up to what God demands. I heard the part during Sunday sermons that labeled me a sinner but missed the part about God's love being unconditional. I surmised incorrectly that if God didn't love me, how could anyone ever love me? After reaching another level of honesty, I finally saw that it was me who was doing the rejection. I conjured the "God doesn't love me" lie to avoid having to surrender completely to God's will. God is love. All I had to do was accept it. And strangely, once I accepted His love, I was able to do His will.

> Not many people can truthfully assert that they love everybody. Most of us must admit that we have loved but a few; that we have been quite indifferent to the many so long as none of them gave us trouble; and as for the remainder— well, we have really disliked or hated them.
> *Alcoholics Anonymous World Service, Inc. Twelve Steps and Twelve Traditions (p. 92). AA World Services, Inc.*

When my relationships failed, it was because I was still trying to live my life my way. I used to whine that I was incapable of love. And even worse, I used the notion that I was unlovable to keep from surrendering to God. I wanted to be in control. I wanted to call the shots. I wanted to be God.

I said I loved God, but I thought more about myself than I ever really thought about God. It was conditional love on my part. Even my prayers were selfish. I would pray for specific outcomes rather than for God's will for me. If I got what I wanted, I took the credit, and if I didn't get what I wanted, I interpreted it as another instance of God not loving me. My theory on love boiled down to "I said the words I love you, but in my heart, it was more quid pro quo than agape."

> But how many men and women speak love with their lips, and believe what they say, so that they can hide lust in a dark corner of their minds?
> *Alcoholics Anonymous World Service, Inc. Twelve Steps and Twelve Traditions (p. 67). AA World Services, Inc.*

This twisted notion also explains why I was unwilling and unable to love others. I said things I thought I meant, but just below the surface, I hid a selfish motive. If you called me on it, I would feign indignation. How could you think such a thing? If our relationship failed, I first blamed you and then I blamed God.

I have a friend who challenges me to transition from my head to my heart. I can see him pointing to his head and then to his heart. He says that this short distance may be only a few inches, but for an alcoholic, it can be an imponderable span. He implied that I had an intellectual understanding of God, but I fell short of feeling His presence. Instead of a God of my understanding, I had a God of my misunderstanding.

It wasn't until I got into AA and completed the Twelve Steps that I came to love and be loved. I now know that God loves me unconditionally, and I have come to love myself. I love myself, warts and all. And others love me unconditionally as well. Without this level of love, I am lost. Without it, I am useless to myself and to others. Without this mature love, I am unable to think of anyone other than myself, let alone to be of service to anyone else.

I am not cured of this emotional malady. But now I know better. If I would happen to interact with someone else under the pretense of love, it more than likely falls short in the eye of the beholder. They see it for what it is: a smoke screen to get something I want or a defense to keep something I'm afraid I'll lose. So even if I check my motives for true love, without God, I surrender to my ancient enemy: rationalization. I begin to justify my selfish motives and fall short of God's standard for love.

God is the source of all true love. Once I accept the certainty of God's love for me and feel it without reservation, I am able to start loving myself. Once I love myself as one of God's children, I am able to care about others. Caring for others is the key that opens the portal to true love. It is only then I will begin to understand the Bible's admonition to love my neighbor as myself. I want change. I will strive to genuinely care about others.

> The idea that we can be possessively loving of a few, can ignore the many, and can continue to fear or hate anybody, has to be abandoned, if only a little at a time.
> *Alcoholics Anonymous World Service, Inc. Twelve Steps and Twelve Traditions (pp. 92–93). AA World Services, Inc.*

This attitude of caring doesn't work if it is manufactured out of a sense of duty. I have been guilty of last-minute gifts or cards to loved ones. They were sometimes given without much thought or genuine affection. I did it to dissuade guilt over not acknowledging a personal event where something special was expected. It didn't work. Often, it rang hollow because it was not given with genuine care.

Caring for others finally happened because of my personal transformation. I started to feel better about doing things for others because I was no longer doing them from any sense of obligation. This happened after the spiritual awakening I had when I successfully completed the Twelve Steps of Alcoholics Anonymous. God permitted this new authenticity, which I lacked in relationships. He really was doing for me what I could not do for myself. Today I now know what true love is. How is it manifested? It is shown in service to others. It is not shown in what I say but what I do. For instance, I may say I love you, but you will believe it when I show you. When I transitioned from "self-centered to the extreme" to becoming "selflessly helpful," love *compelled* me to give back what I was so freely given. Out of love, I became willing to serve.

Can I serve without any expectation for anything in return? Am I willing to sacrifice my time and interests to serve others? I'm no Mother

Teresa, but she is the person who comes to mind as one who was able to give so selflessly.

She is known for aiding the poorest of the poor. She dedicated her life to love, sacrifice, and service. It's hard to imagine that level of dedication and commitment. She cast aside the worldly comforts for herself and pushed aside any of the comforts that so many pursue. She had to be spiritually awake beyond anything I will ever achieve. She was a saint. I am not, but I strive to grow along spiritual lines.

There are numerous members of AA who may have a spiritual experience sufficient for them to keep sober, but have they had a spiritual awakening? Yet there are those in AA that I look up to for their spirituality. These individuals have had a change of heart, mind, and spirit, and it shows. Their whole demeanor cries out that they have been transformed. These are the folks who willingly sacrifice their time and talent to do the work necessary to grow the fellowship and keep the AA traditions alive. They serve others in and out of the program in a way that is sacrificial and selfless. As I mentally review names and faces in AA, I can think of several who are so dedicated.

During the pandemic, I spent much time at home due to the coronavirus pandemic. I was blessed to be able to connect with other alcoholics via Zoom meetings, which satisfied my need for fellowship. During one of those meetings, I reconnected with an alcoholic who manages a restaurant. I could see that he was busy preparing food just prior to a mandated closure of his business. Even though this had to be worrisome for him and his employees, his focus was on how to get the food he had to those in need. He shared during those Zoom meetings that he would be willing to drop off food to anyone who might be in need. Others in the meeting shared about their fear and challenges, but this man was totally focused on the needs of others, and he seemed joyful for the opportunity. Miraculous!

I can think of another gentleman who came to my Monday night meeting years ago with practically nothing. He was unemployable and without hope. He was also illiterate. He was introduced to the Big Book of Alcoholics Anonymous. He couldn't read it, but with the help of his sponsor, he memorized large portions of the first 164 pages. He kept on studying the Big Book with his sponsor and miraculously taught himself to read. He is now an evangelist for the program. He not only reads, but he is on fire with the joy that comes from a spiritual experience. He has sponsored countless alcoholics who, like him, had no hope. Now his sponsees are also on fire for the solution and are carrying the message that was so freely and enthusiastically shared. Miraculous!

I worked with a man who came to the program full of anger and resentment, and he did not assimilate easily. In fact, I could go so far to say he was antisocial. Three police showed up during one of his first meetings, and they knew him from previous encounters. He seemed to fight everything and everybody and was quick to point out the hypocrisy he saw. But he did not drink. He gravitated to the Big Book study tables, and although he still has a penchant for criticism, he has stayed sober. He completed all the steps and dedicated himself to AA. I believe he attended over 1100 meetings in his first eighteen months in addition to significant outside research with lectures and online investigation. The result? He is not only still sober, but he also takes on newcomers others would not help. He is relentless and never gives up on anyone. He desperately wants them to have the solution he has found. Miraculous!

There is another young lady who early in AA was slipping and sliding (drinking again) and could not seem to get the program, even though she was highly intelligent and had graduated with a degree from a prestigious university. She would come to the meetings high and mostly just tried to blend in. But she kept coming back to the meetings. Eventually she read a passage in the Big Book that seemed to be her tipping point.

> We, in our turn, sought the same escape with all the desperation of drowning men. What seemed at first a flimsy reed, has proved to be the loving and powerful hand of God. A new life has been given us or, if you prefer, "a design for living" that really works. *Inc, AA World Services. Alcoholics Anonymous, 4th ed. (p. 28). AA World Services, Inc.*

She is now employed and has a very responsible position with her company. She is extremely active in AA. She sponsors people and takes them through the Twelve Steps. She is active in AA district and regional committees and is scheduling visits to women's prisons, all while parenting two active children and supporting her husband. She does it all joyfully and is an example to us all. Miraculous!

There is another woman who finds time beyond her busy schedule as nurse and mother to head up many meetings and sponsor many alcoholics. She is a student of the Big Book and defender of the AA Twelve Traditions. She is very active with AA council committees and is a resource to meetings who need assistance getting back to our singleness of purpose. She does it tirelessly and with great joy. Miraculous!

This willingness to serve seems to be a common characteristic of recovered alcoholics. Many alcoholics are compelled to a life of service. For them, it is more than just a nice thing to do occasionally. It has become a mainstay of what they do to keep their life free from drugs and alcohol.

Bill Wilson heard this from his friend Ebby. Ebby had been one of his drinking buddies and now was in his kitchen telling him what he had to do to stay sober.

> My friend had emphasized the absolute necessity of demonstrating these principles in all my affairs. Particularly was it imperative to work with others as he had worked with me. Faith without works was dead, he said. And how appallingly true for the alcoholic! For if an alcoholic failed to perfect and enlarge his spiritual life through work and self-sacrifice for others, he could not survive the certain trials and low spots ahead. If he did not work, he would surely drink again, and if he drank, he would surely die. Then faith would be dead indeed.
>
> *Inc, AA World Services. Alcoholics Anonymous, 4th ed. (pp. 14–15). AA World Services, Inc.*

A life of service starts with a mindset. I now choose to add to the world rather than take from it. It is just as simple as looking for the opportunities and then offering to help. Just by saying something like "Do you have a Big Book? Do you have a sponsor?" Even after something as simple as these questions, the door can open to a freedom from self that leads to lifelong friendships.

There is another feature of this willingness to serve that a friend of mine recently stressed. He says, "I try to do the right thing for someone else without getting caught." Remaining anonymous assures that my motives are right and that I am doing things without expecting anything in return. Doing the next right thing becomes its own reward and reinforces my desire and intention to do God's will. The Bible confirms the need for anonymity.

> But when you give to the needy, do not let your left hand know what your right hand is doing, so that your giving may be in secret. Then your Father, who sees what is done in secret, will reward you. (Matthew 6:3–4 NSV)

Love and service to others certainly must be an important part of *live and let live*. But could it lead to more? Perhaps it could lead not only to *live and let live* but *love and let love*.

Humility

> "Absolute humility," said AA co-founder Bill W., "would consist of a state of complete freedom from myself, freedom from all the claims that my defects of character now lay so heavily upon me. Perfect humility would be a full willingness, in all times and places, to find and to do the will of God."

I will never achieve humility with any degree of perfection. I will continue to strive for it. I have heard it said that humility is the goal of all the Twelve Steps of AA. While I agree that this is true, I often get humility confused with humiliation. Clearly, there is a distinction. I am not asked to wear sackcloth and ashes and fall into morbidity and self-flagellation.

> Where humility had formerly stood for a forced feeding on humble pie, it now begins to mean the nourishing ingredient which can give us serenity.
> *Alcoholics Anonymous World Service, Inc. Twelve Steps and Twelve Traditions (p. 74). AA World Services, Inc.*

Humility opens the portal to a God consciousness that leads to peace of mind and serenity. It is the faith that "God really is doing for me that I cannot do for myself." It is the realization of what I hoped to get from the first three steps of AA. As I have heard many times in AA meetings, those three steps can be distilled to "I can't, God can, and I'll let Him." But this needs to be more than an elective journey; it is core to survival itself. Without humility, there is no hope of ever remaining sober. Without sobriety, there is no hope of becoming a useful member of society.

> For without some degree of humility, no alcoholic can stay sober at all. Nearly all AA's have found, too, that unless they develop much more of this precious quality than may be required just for sobriety, they still haven't much chance of becoming truly happy. Without it, they cannot live to much useful purpose, or, in adversity, be able to summon the faith that can meet any emergency.
> *Alcoholics Anonymous World Service, Inc. Twelve Steps and Twelve Traditions (p. 70). AA World Services, Inc.*

Bill Wilson had his challenges with humility, but he concluded that humility is not a "sentence" but a "blessing." It takes work to get there and even more work and discipline to stay there. He had to work for it.

> So it is that we first see humility as a necessity. But this is the barest beginning. To get completely away from our aversion to the idea of being humble, to gain a vision of humility as the avenue to true freedom of the human spirit, to be willing to work for humility as something to be desired for itself, takes most of us a long, long time. A whole lifetime geared to self-centeredness cannot be set in reverse all at once. Rebellion dogs our every step at first.
> *Alcoholics Anonymous World Service, Inc. Twelve Steps and Twelve Traditions*

After our son was born and even before I got sober, I was quite active in my church. I really wanted to achieve the spirituality that I saw in others. I wanted to want it, but something was missing. Even earlier as a teenager, I remember the pastor would call congregants to come forward during a service to publicly share a commitment to a life with Christ. I wondered at the time why so many people were crying. Why were they so sad? I just didn't get it. Back then, I doubt whether I really wanted to understand it. These crying folks were trying to divest themselves from the temptations and clamors of the world, and I was eager to grab all that they were divesting. This attitude diminished somewhat over the years as I became a member of one congregation or another. There were times I thought I had it during a particularly moving sermon, a poignant hymn, or a moving choral presentation. Finally, in AA I came to understand that I would never be able to have an authentic spiritual experience in church or anywhere else until I truly humbled myself.

> We supposed we had humility when really we hadn't. We supposed we had been serious about religious practices when, upon honest appraisal, we found we had been only superficial. Or, going to the other extreme, we had wallowed in emotionalism and had mistaken it for true religious feeling. In both cases, we had been asking something for nothing. The fact was we really hadn't cleaned house so that the grace of God could enter us and expel the obsession. In no deep or meaningful sense had we ever taken stock of ourselves, made amends to those we had harmed, or freely given to any other human being without any demand for reward. We had not even prayed rightly. We had always said, "Grant me my wishes" instead of "Thy will be done." The love of God and man we understood not at all. Therefore we remained self-deceived, and so incapable of receiving enough grace to restore us to sanity.
> *Alcoholics Anonymous World Service, Inc. Twelve Steps and Twelve Traditions (p. 32). AA World Services, Inc.*

The seventh step in AA tells me to "humbly ask God to remove my defects of character." I can't hide from God. He knows every hair on my head. He knows my every thought and action. If I really want to know God and have a relationship with Him, He wants me to identify and acknowledge my defects of character. The eternal relationship with God my Creator begins now and not some distant point in the future when I die and must face God. I don't want to live with just enough spirituality to make the cut getting into heaven. I want a relationship with God now. I want Him to help me see the things in my life that do not conform to His will for me. I want to own up to the selfish worldly distractions that keep me from being useful and happy. My prayer is for God to remove these shortcomings and be granted knowledge and strength to do His will.

> For just so long as we were convinced that we could live exclusively by our own individual strength and intelligence, for just that long was a working faith in a Higher Power impossible. This was true even when we believed that God existed. We could actually have earnest religious beliefs which remained barren because we were still trying to play God ourselves. As long as we placed self-reliance first, a genuine reliance upon a Higher Power was out of the question. That basic ingredient of all humility, a desire to seek and do God's will, was missing.
> *Alcoholics Anonymous World Service Inc ... Twelve Steps and Twelve Traditions (p. 72). AA World Services, Inc.*

I have witnessed people in AA who have had real humility. But like me, many of my fellow AAs often slip back into periods of selfishness and self-centeredness. Humility as a virtue is difficult to attain and even harder to keep.

There was an alcoholic I recall from early in my sobriety who had more humility than most. Ironically, he called himself "humble Jack." He had a booming voice and at one time must have been a mountain of a man. He would start each of his shares during the meetings with "Hi, I'm humble Jack, and I am a *reeeeeeeeeal* alcoholic." He was wheelchair bound, but he remained tall. He was an imposing force, not because of his physicality but because of his spirituality.

When I first saw him at meetings, I felt pity for him. Over time, I couldn't see the wheelchair. It slipped away somehow. The chair was always there, but it faded away, hidden by the perpetual smile pasted on his face. He had a quiet serenity that was contagious. His whole demeanor and deportment shouted gratitude and recovery. I never once heard him complain or whine. He always talked about what he did each day to stay sober and how much he loved AA. How could a man with his afflictions be so positive? How could he not focus on his dilemma? Why was he more interested in helping others than wallowing in self-pity? He may have had physical afflictions, but his spiritual house was in order. He epitomized the virtues of "live and let live." He accepted his dis-ease and demonstrated to the rest of us that humility really could be achieved. When I get to heaven and am welcomed into the big AA meeting in the sky, I bet that humble Jack will be there to greet me. He'll say, "My name is Jack, and I'm a *reeeeeeeeeeeal* alcoholic." And the angels will sing.

Suppression of Unhealthy Demands upon Others

I have often shared that I do not care what other people think of me. I have said that other people's opinion of me is none of my business. I once heard another friend sing the first verse of a song, "If you don't happen to like me, pass me by."

The song speaks of going it alone, being able to pick and choose what the world and the people in it have to offer. If I don't like any of it, I am free, and so are they, to move on. It sounds appealing not to have to worry about what other people think and to have the ability to go my own way, comfortable with my own choices. I would then be truly free. Then I really could wear the world around me like a loose cloak. I could release the things that bind or constrict me and toss them off. I could go through life comfortable in my own skin with boundaries that would cause me to bend to the whim or will of others. Isn't this what being truly independent with a healthy sense of self is all about? Wouldn't I then be able to live and let live?

There may be a flaw in this logic. It could be selfish. It could imply that everything is about me, what I want, and what I need. This inordinate focus on self is a contributor to my disease. It could be the justification of a focus on self and self alone. I would have to reconcile this with the truth of how I relate to others. Like Bill Wilson, I am likely going to have unhealthy dependencies. I will either work feverishly to earn others love and respect, cost what it may, or I may try to dominate them to make them conform to my will. This is the dilemma for an alcoholic. Either I'm on top of the heap, struggling to keep everyone beneath me subservient, or I'm underneath the pile, hiding from view while simultaneously hoping someone will rescue me.

> Our egomania digs two disastrous pitfalls. Either we insist upon dominating the people we know, or we depend upon them far too much. If we lean too heavily on people, they will sooner or later fail us, for they are human, too, and cannot possibly meet our incessant demands. In this way our insecurity grows and festers. When we habitually try to manipulate others to our own willful desires, they revolt, and resist us heavily. Then we develop hurt feelings, a sense of persecution, and a desire to retaliate. As we redouble our efforts at control, and continue to fail, our suffering becomes acute and constant.
>
> Alcoholics Anonymous World Service, Inc. *Twelve Steps and Twelve Traditions (p. 53)*. AA World Services, Inc.

I really do want to fit in and get along with others, but I am no longer willing to go to any lengths to do so. I have found that some associations are not healthy. For those individuals, the Bible suggests that I should give them three chances, and after the third interaction that is harmful to me, I should let them go. Or as the Al-Anons say, "Release them with love." I don't need to keep trying to chase anyone who cannot or will not give me a modicum of respect. I have heard others say they protect themselves from the unreasonable demands of others by setting boundaries. I would agree that this is a healthy way to remain engaged with others without sacrificing my values and integrity. But what about my unreasonable demands of others and my need for approval, adulation, and attention? Like Bill Wilson, I have not always been able to be less dependent. I now know in my heart that my perfectionistic demands of others are not healthy for them or myself.

> My basic flaw had always been dependence—almost absolute dependence—on people or circumstances to supply me with prestige, security, and the like. (Bill Wilson)

I need a strategy to use when faced with situations and relationships requiring honest judgment and healthy communication. I am writing this book in part to identify and apply tools I can use to relieve myself from unhealthy dependencies.

Positive Attitude

I had a coworker who used to say that a positive attitude can win anyone over in all situations. He would ask groups he led in meetings to join him in placing their hands in a triangle and have them say in unison, "Attitude!" He would then have them point to another team member and say, "Make yours." And finally he would have them make a plus sign with their index fingers and say in unison, "Positive!"

Reactions varied, but eventually groups lightened up and were receptive to the messages for positivity in the workplace. I was less receptive. I thought the whole thing was hokey and beneath my sensibilities. I had a negative attitude. I would smile while I heard these over-the-top attempts at motivation, and I was embarrassed for my friend for what I thought would be a highly negative and sarcastic response. I thought the whole glad-handing, smile-your-way-into-a-superficial connection could never be real or even necessary.

Oh, and I was drinking heavily at the time. I was unwilling to consider the pursuit of positivity. I used to tell my friend when he questioned my negativity, "Yeah, I have a positive attitude. I'm positive I'm negative!" I thought it was hilarious. He never laughed. He would just smile and shake his head.

At that time, I professed to be a Christian, and I really did believe that Jesus was my Savior, but I thought it was to be kept personal and be reserved for church and worship. I really didn't feel like it was anybody else's business.

Speaking again of my coworker friend, he had his challenges in a relationship that ended in divorce. We were doing training sessions in another state, which included after hour drinking and opportunities to let our hair down. We followed the unwritten maxims of business that suggested that we should work hard and play hard.

It wasn't too long after that when we traveled back to the home office with another associate who also was a devout Christian. My associate was quite open about his faith. He wanted to introduce my coworker friend to a woman who had special spiritual gifts. I was curious but at the same time quite skeptical. I tagged along unconvinced that there would be anyone who legitimately could affect anyone's spiritual condition. I expected to find a fortune-teller, not a prophet.

When we met with this woman, I had to admit there was something otherworldly about her. Her eyes were piercing and deep. She looked into my friend's eyes and took his hands in hers. She told him that God had a great plan for him in his life if he would listen for God's calling. I don't remember the exact words as much as the feeling, but something happened to my friend that day. It was a transformation. Coworkers used to call him the "prince of darkness." And now he had the same otherworldly look about him that suggested he had found religion.

Shortly after, he joined a church, married the love of his life, and became a very sought-after speaker and business coach. He became very active in men's ministry. The mystery woman was correct. God did have a great plan for his life. I should have paid closer attention to what was happening.

It didn't happen that miraculously for me, but because of AA and successful completion of the Twelve Steps, I have had a spiritual awakening. I must also admit that while I have had a change of heart, my attitude has taken its sweet time in becoming positive. There will be more work and faith required for that progression.

They told me in the program that the promises happen sometimes quickly and sometimes slowly but that they will always materialize if we work for them. I believe that one of the causes for my slow transition had to do with where I was putting my focus. I focused chiefly on ridding myself of my character defects and failed to enlarge my character assets. I am focusing today not so much on where I fell short as I am on the attributes I am striving to attain.

Part of my morning prayer routine for years has included asking my Higher Power to remove several character flaws. I pray that He will help me watch out for selfishness, dishonesty, resentment, and fear. When—not if—these defects crop up, I ask God to remove them. I am then to discuss this with someone immediately and make amends quickly if I have harmed anyone. Then I need to resolutely turn my thoughts to someone I can help. Love and tolerance of others is to be my code. And while I know that God wants me to work to be free of my character flaws, I now believe that I should also pray for positive replacements. I will pray for character strengths. Additionally, if the passage in the Big Book about acceptance says that "the only thing I can change is me and my attitudes," I had also better start praying for a positive attitude.

Bottom line is what I strive for tends to grow. It's a variation on the Native American tale of two wolves. Imagine two wolves. One wants nothing good for me and constantly fuels my negativity. The other wants what is right and good for me and fuels my positivity. Which one prevails? The one I feed.

I heard another story recently that speaks to my need for being positive. There was an alcoholic who moved to a new town and visited his first AA meeting. Before the meeting, he was having a cup of coffee and was greeted by one of the regulars. He struck up a conversation, which eventually led to asking, "What are the people like in this meeting?" The other alcoholic questioned, "What were they like in the meetings you went to in your old town?" The new alcoholic thought for a while and said, "They were not very open. They were cliquish and not very welcoming to newcomers. They talked the talk, but they didn't walk the walk." The other alcoholic responded with "Yeah, they're like that here as well."

After a week or so, another alcoholic moved to the same town and visited the meeting for the first time. He struck up a conversation with the same alcoholic who had greeted the visitor a week prior. Eventually the new visitor asked the same question. "What are the people like in this meeting?" And the alcoholic asked, "What were they like where you are from?" The visitor responded, "They were very friendly. They welcomed newcomers and were active in service. They were working the program and practicing the principles in all of their affairs." The other alcoholic responded, "Yeah, they're like that here."

Like my son told me lately, "You will find what you are looking for!" I need to look for the good in everyone with whom I come in contact. The Big Book says, "When I complain about you or me, I am complaining about God's creation." We are all children of God, and I am discovering that looking for the best in others is essential if I am to live and let live.

Healthy Relationships

Emotional well-being depends on my ability to get along with others. This seems foundational for my goal to live and let live. If I am to enjoy healthy relationships, I must be healthy physically, emotionally, and spiritually. I can't give away or share what I do not have. This has always been a tall order. Others I have known have picked up on this self-love concept naturally. For me, it has been anything but natural. Whatever the misshapen and neurotic reasons might be, I have never been able get in touch with my "healthy self-image" gene. No more excuses. It's time for me to be OK with who I am and who I'm becoming with God's help.

The Bible tells me to love my neighbor as myself. My neighbor will never get much love until I can love and respect myself. This includes a wholistic inclusion of body, mind, and spirit. It starts with taking care of my body. The Bible tells me that my body is my temple. I am told to not defile my temple physically or morally. I can improve my health by eating right and exercising. A friend once told me that my body is God's gift to me and how I take care of my body is my gift to God. I recently made the decision to lose over forty pounds with the help of another recovering alcoholic. I feel significantly better and believe I am healthier overall. All glory to God!

I must also feed my mental and spiritual health and become mentally strong and morally straight. I must strive to be independent and not be a burden on those I would befriend. My sense of self includes protecting my core values and beliefs, which I will not compromise or sacrifice. This requires that I finally be able to set boundaries and protect myself from being bullied, used, or abused. If I have the integrity of genuine self-love, I will then be able to love others as myself. Once I can love myself, then I am ready to meet the ABCs of three basic needs that all healthy relationships must satisfy:

> ➤ acceptance: permitting those I love to be themselves
> ➤ being attentive: devotion, affection, fondness
> ➤ caring: emotional support; sympathy, empathy, listening

Getting along with others and ultimately being able to live and let live requires more than I can do on my own. Without help it is too much for me. I need to rely less on selfish insight and rely more on guidance from the Holy Spirit.

I recently saw an ad for a religious organization on TV that depicted several scenarios where one or more of the people in each of the scenes were downtrodden, depressed, angry, or frustrated. One of the scenes showed a person bent over, tie askew, looking disheveled as he literally dragged himself to the front door of his home. He was clearly exhausted and used up. Suddenly, there appeared to be a swirling force descending on him before he went through the front door and, instead of greeting his family in a negative state, he crossed the threshold reenergized and smiling. Another scene showed two drivers stalled in traffic, and after one of the drivers blasts his horn, the other driver responds in kind and they begin pumping their fists and yelling at each other. The same swirling force seemed to descend on one and then the other and the anger dissolved and was replaced by greetings of good will and harmony.

I admit that I have relied on the false notion that if others would behave better, then I would too. Has that ever worked for me? No. I must focus on the Holy Spirit to keep me willing and able to interact more positively. Like a familiar song suggests, "Let there be peace on earth, and let it begin with me."

It is my personal relationships, particularly my marriage, where I must be particularly attentive. I have been told that marital relationships should be a 50/50 affair. I have learned the hard way that the relationships I want to nurture require me to give more than my share. If emotional support and validation are essential to good relationships, then I need to devote the time and quality attention they deserve. I must demonstrate that attention by showing care and concern in a way that is genuinely meaningful to the recipient. This is particularly essential with my wife. I never want to hear, "You don't love me anymore." If that ever happens, it means my daily attention went wanting. I didn't actively provide evidence of how much I care for her. This attentive state means that I must be the one to be accountable for picking up on the cues my wife provides without having to be prompted or reminded.

It really is the little things, sincerely offered, that communicate my love. Positive gestures and inclusive dialogue help reinforce my desire to sustain a relationship. Gary Chapman, in his book *Five Love Languages*, shares the following five ways that we can connect:

1. words of affirmation
2. quality time
3. receiving gifts
4. acts of service
5. physical touch

I have learned in over five decades of marriage that my wife's love language preferences are words of affirmation, quality time, and acts of service. It's not that the others are not important, but if I fall short on these top three preferences, I am not as attentive as she requires. I need to carve out time for her, to be available to talk and be with her. I need to tell her how much I love and care for her. I can no longer assume that somehow she will just know how I feel about her. I now know I need to look for ways to be helpful around the house. I need to take care of the obvious areas that require attention without being nagged to do so.

My friends also need attention. Friendship is precious. I need to text, phone, visit, and spend the time to include them in my daily life. There must be some evidence of just how important they are to me.

I must earn my friends' respect. That means I must keep my word and keep my commitments. If I say I am going to do something, I must do it. That kind of commitment wasn't evident in some of my lesser associations. If something better came up for them, they wouldn't honor their commitment. They would say, "Something came up." I would say, "OK, maybe next time," knowing full well that it was another slip in the knot that joined us.

Another opportunity to show respect occurs when I can go to bat for a friend. If another person starts talk negatively about my friend, am I willing to intervene on my friend's behalf? Am I willing to avoid gossip about my friend? After all, if I really know a person, I am going to know the good, the bad, and even sometimes the ugly. Am I willing to see the relationship as a package deal, accepting them for who and what they really are and not just what I would like them to be?

I am now willing to do the work to save relationships and let bygones be bygones. This requires me to forgive and forget. I am willing to swallow my pride and ask for forgiveness when I have said or done something that I regret. However, I have learned that forgiveness is nearly impossible when I am not in fit spiritual condition. I am learning that making amends involves more than a casual "I'm sorry." It includes sharing my regrets for harms done along with my intent for new and better behavior in the future. What keeps me from forgiveness? For me, it's selfish pride. Because I am unwilling to swallow my pride, I will fight to the bitter end to defend my position rather than surrender to God's will, which requires me to love others as myself.

Healthy relationships respect their effort made to grow and mature. For instance, if a good friend is taking a class on a subject or new interest, it is important for me to take interest and acknowledge their accomplishment.

If my spouse is seeing a psychiatrist or psychologist to identify and expel demons of the past, I had better be supportive and show genuine interest.

If I am sincerely trying to clean up my language or offer more help around the house, it helps to be recognized for the effort.

On the other hand, if only one person in the relationship is doing the work to grow the relationship, then at a minimum it may be time for an adult conversation about the state of the union.

Emotional Independence

"To thine own self be true" can be found on one side of coins passed out in AA to celebrate various milestones of recovery. I cannot depend on anyone else for my happiness. I cannot make anyone else happy, nor can others make me happy. The program tells me that happiness is an inside job.

I am responsible for naming and owning my feelings. Before AA, the only emotions I felt were anger and fear. Since completing the AA steps, I am now experiencing the full gamut of emotions that normal people feel. When I am asked, "How does that make you feel?" I strive to be honest with myself and own my feelings. I am working on being able to communicate how I feel without any additional rancor or inappropriate histrionics.

Overreacting is a habit that I am trying to break. I must be willing to let the slings and arrows of perceived attacks be filtered with rational thoughts. So rather than overreact to a perceived assault, I need to pause and reflect before I respond. This is true for all conversations, face-to-face or virtual.

I admit that I have often sat in silent scorn when I didn't like the circumstances I faced. When the other person involved would say something like "What's going on with you? You seem upset!" I would react with folded arms and frowning face while saying nothing. This was, and sometimes is, a hangover from my childish pouting days. In my early days working with a psychiatrist, after describing some troubling event, I would be asked, "How does that make you feel?" I would say, "I don't know how I feel." Then the psychiatrist would say, "Well, you're the only one who does know."

Learning how to communicate with others and responding appropriately is still a work in progress.

I need to practice responding with "I" rather than "you." For instance, instead of saying, "You never put things away after you use them. When are you ever going to learn?" I might say, "I feel slighted when I find things that were not put back where they belong. I value neatness and appreciate an uncluttered house."

Emotional Maturity

> When I was a child, I talked like a child, I thought like a child, I reasoned like a child. When I became a man, I put the ways of childhood behind me. (1 Corinthians 13:11 NIV)

When I was a child, I couldn't wait until I grew up. I thought that I would no longer have to yield to authority, and then I would be able to do whatever I wanted. The irony of that wish was that it kept me in childishness, or at best adolescence, well into the time I should have been behaving as an adult.

I was late to follow the apostle Paul's admonition to "put away childish things." I know that my alcoholism was complicit in delaying my maturation. Initially, alcohol permitted escape from reality, but over time, it stunted my emotional growth. Someone in AA once shared that whatever age emotionally I was when I started to drink alcoholically would be how old I would be when I stopped. I was in my early twenties when I started drinking alcoholically and stopped when I was forty-one. Does that mean I was still in my early twenties emotionally in my early forties? Yes, and I am working even now to eliminate lingering remnants of that immaturity. That's not to say that there were parts of my life that would look like I was an adult to the casual observer. I had responsible jobs. There were significant promotions, homes, and cars, and my bills were paid. But even when I was drinking, I knew down deep that there was something awry.

I recall a trip to Germany when returning on a long flight I had a conversation with the young lady who sat next to me. She asked me about the book I was reading, *The Peter Pan Syndrome* by the psychologist Dan Kiley. His premise is that for every Peter Pan, there is a Wendy. Peter is the immature, neurotic, wounded, narcissistic boy who never grows up. Enter Wendy. She is the codependent, nurturing caregiver who is more than willing to offer the motherly attention that Peter Pan craves, along with a dose of control that Peter resents. Like Peter, I was stuck in a fantasy world. I preferred relying on my imagination and shamefully often stayed cut off from reality and responsibility. Further research into the nature of narcissists yielded the following list:

> - an exaggerated sense of self-importance
> - a sense of entitlement requiring constant, excessive admiration
> - an expectation to be recognized as superior even without achievements that warrant it
> - exaggeration of achievements and talents

- ▸ preoccupation with fantasies about success, power, brilliance, beauty, or the perfect mate
- ▸ belief that they are superior and can only associate with equally special people
- ▸ monopolization of conversations and belittling or looking down on people they perceive as inferior
- ▸ expectations of special favors and unquestioning compliance with their expectations
- ▸ taking advantage of others to get what they want
- ▸ an inability or unwillingness to recognize the needs and feelings of others
- ▸ envy of others and the belief that others envy them
- ▸ behaving in an arrogant manner and coming across as conceited, boastful, and pretentious
- ▸ insistence on having the best of everything, such as the best car or phone

As fate would have it, for the entire trip we discussed the syndrome and how we may have shared the symptoms of the complex. I discovered that in addition to being an alcoholic I was also a narcissist. I am still amazed at how quickly our neuroses paired us. I was Peter Pan, and she was Wendy. Just a couple of strangers acting out fantasies at 40,000 feet.

The trip must have happened right around the time the book was published. I got sober in 1985, so my insights into my disease as it impacted my emotional well-being must have been starting to bubble to the surface.

I heard a while back that one of the attributes of a mature adult is the ability to defer gratification. I was unable to defer much of anything when I was drinking. I wanted what I wanted, and I wanted it now rather than later. I could be described as childish, overly sensitive, and grandiose. So that unfortunately described who I was, but what about the person I am and the person I am hopefully becoming? With the help of a pamphlet I received from a friend, I prepared a checklist of the characteristics of a person who has achieved true emotional maturity.

Characteristics of Emotional Maturity

Am I able to ...	Yes	No
accept criticism gratefully, being honestly glad for an opportunity to improve?		
not indulge in self-pity and begin to feel the laws of compensation operating in my life?		
not expect special considerations from anyone?		
control my temper?		
meet emergencies with poise?		
acknowledge that my feelings are not easily hurt?		
accept responsibility of my own acts without trying to alibi?		
outgrow the "all or nothing" stage and recognize that no person or situation is wholly good or wholly bad? And begin to appreciate the golden mean (desirable middle between two extremes)?		
not be impatient at reasonable delays? And learn that I am not the arbiter of the universe and that I must often adjust myself to other people and their convenience?		
be a good loser? Can I endure defeat and disappointment without whining or complaining?		
not boast or show off in socially unacceptable ways?		
be honestly glad when others enjoy success or good fortune?		
outgrow envy and jealousy?		
be open-minded enough to listen thoughtfully to the opinions of others?		
not be a chronic faultfinder?		
plan things in advance rather than trusting to the inspiration of the moment?		

As I review my answers, I must admit there is still room for improvement for the emotional maturity I seek. I am not going to beat myself up over it though. I am relying on God for the impetus to change and the willingness to grow in a direction He desires.

I am grateful to the fellow AA who contributed their thoughts and reactions in response to Bill Wilson's letter to the *Grapevine* on emotional sobriety. Like Bill, I feel as though I have identified many of the flawed characteristics he shared even after a significant recovery time. And while I have already shared some of my perceptions and experience with the behaviors necessary to grow emotionally, I will explore what more is available to help me grow toward my goal of emotional sobriety.

4

Emotional Intelligence

What Is Emotional Intelligence?

Emotional intelligence (EQ) was originated by two psychologists, John Mayer, and Peter Salovey. I read a book written in 1995 by Daniel Coleman entitled *Emotional Intelligence: Why It Can Matter More than IQ.* This book explains how emotions and feelings can be just as powerful as intellect and logic in determining outcomes and living successfully in a modern world. It accounts for how emotions and intellect can coexist, and it suggests how the balance between the two can guide us or affect us.

How Does EQ differ from IQ?

How does EQ differ from IQ? I have heard the difference explained as simply as IQ gets you through school, and EQ gets you through life. IQ measures the ability to reason, assimilate facts and use logic. EQ measures our intuition, empathy, stress management capacities, resilience, and integrity.

A person is born with whatever IQ they will possess. It lasts throughout their lifetime and cannot be changed. EQ can be changed, and for the better. And studies show the higher the EQ, the more successful a person can be.

I can think of a perfect example of having a high IQ is just not enough to get by in the world. My example appeared in a TV show called *The Big Bang Theory*. It was very popular as is its spinoff called *Young Sheldon*. Both shows feature a character called Sheldon Cooper. The spinoff features Sheldon as a young teenager growing up in Texas. He is a genius and while he excels without equal at math and science, he lacks both social and life skills. His heroes are theoretical physicists and mathematicians. His fictional hero is Mr. Spock from *Star Trek*. Here is the kind of logic that typifies why Sheldon identified with Mr. Spock.

> May I say that I have not thoroughly enjoyed serving with humans? I find their illogic and foolish emotions a constant irritant. *(Star Trek,* season 3, episode 7, "Day of the Dove," 1968)

Sheldon's IQ is in the stratosphere, but his EQ hovers in a lower quartile. Perhaps it's because of this dichotomy that the show was a comedic hit, even though at times it is a little sad. The angst exists due to the gap that exists between his intellectual and social skills. Here's an example:

> There's no denying I have feelings for you that can't be explained away in any other way. I briefly considered that I had a brain parasite, but that seems even more far-fetched. The only conclusion was love. (Sheldon from *The Big Bang Theory)*

Growing emotionally never seemed to register with Sheldon. I, on the other hand, desire to grow emotionally. I am exploring the tenets of emotional intelligence with the hope it will provide insights in my quest for emotional integrity and maturity.

Online Testing for EQ

The desire to relate better with others while remaining true to myself and my values seems like a worthwhile outcome to pursue. Where am

I on the EQ scale? I took an online test offered through the *Psychology Today* web site (www.psychologytoday.com/us/tests/personality/ emotional-intelligence-test).

Overall, I was surprised with the results.

Summary

This emotional intelligence test consists of two parts: a self-report portion and an ability portion. The test assesses your capacity to recognize your own emotions and those of others, understand how best to motivate yourself, become close to others, and manage your own feelings and those of others.

Overall Results
EQ score = 124; percentile score = 95

Your score on this assessment is fairly good. Overall, you are quite capable of understanding and dealing with emotions. Review the rest of your results to know which areas you might need to work on developing.

I was tested for

- emotional identification, perception, and expression
- emotional facilitation of thought
- emotional understanding
- emotional management
- ego maturity (including twenty-seven subcategories)

I excelled in problem-solving, conflict management knowledge, and emotional selectivity. I had limitations in impulse control and flexibility. Almost all the other categories have room for improvement, and the report offered specific descriptors of what I'll need to do.

You don't need to take the time for a test. You can get a quick sense of how much growth may be needed for EQ by taking stock of the following descriptors of EQ challenges:

1. **You get stressed easily.** When you stuff your feelings, they quickly build into the uncomfortable sensations of tension, stress, and anxiety. Unaddressed emotions strain the mind and body. People who fail to use their emotional intelligence skills are more likely to turn to other, less effective means of managing their mood. They are twice as likely to experience anxiety, depression, substance abuse, and even thoughts of suicide.

2. **You have difficulty asserting yourself.** When most people are crossed, they default to passive or aggressive behavior.

3. **You have a limited emotional vocabulary.** All people experience emotions, but it is a select few who can accurately identify them as they occur. Research shows that only one out of three people can do this. Unlabeled emotions often go misunderstood. This might lead to irrational choices and unintended consequences.

4. **You make assumptions quickly and then defend them vehemently.** People who lack EQ form an opinion quickly without considering other options. They then defend their choice.

5. **You hold grudges.** For alcoholics, grudges lead to resentments, and resentments are "the number one offender." Grudges lead to stress, and stress affects health and well-being.

6. **You don't let go of mistakes.** Letting go of mistakes reduces anxiety. Learn from them, and then let them go.

7. **You often feel misunderstood.** You have difficulty delivering your message in a way that people can understand.

8. **You don't know your triggers.** If you can identify your triggers, you can work to respond more appropriately.

9. **You don't get angry.** Pollyanna behavior and stuffing anger are not healthy or honest.

10. **You blame other people for how they make you feel.** You become a victim. Emotions come from within. Others can only affect your feelings if you let them. You are responsible for the way you feel.

11. **You're easily offended.** If you have a healthy self-concept, what other people say or do will not affect you so negatively.

Bringing It All Together

I desire to develop new habits to replace old habits that limit or block emotional growth. I want to eliminate old, destructive behaviors.

Here are some of my actions I will take to improve my emotional intelligence. I will

> balance good manners, empathy, and kindness with my efforts to assert myself and establish boundaries
> better master my emotions
> let my thoughts marinate, evolving from emotions that limit growth and move to rational thoughts that are more appropriate for relational growth
> avoid holding onto stress at all costs
> catch on when people don't understand what I am saying, then adjust my approach and recommunicate in a way that can be understood
> spot and tackle tough situations before things escalate
> study my triggers and sidestep situations and people before they get the best of me
> employ negative and positive emotions intentionally but also appropriately in all situations
> take responsibility for my emotions and develop more useful methods to let others know how I feel
> be open-minded and willing to consider other points of view
> be less offended and avoid resentments at all costs
> stop taking things so personally

Leaning into EQ

It is one thing to know what to do and perhaps get the right answers if I am taking some sort of EQ test. The jury is out on that regard. And even after learning the new approaches, will I be able to apply what I am learning into real-life situations? Sometimes in the heat of the moment I may revert to old behaviors that didn't work before and likely will never work.

Here are a couple of examples of possible dialogues that show the before and after with some of the EQ principles in mind.

Childish Husband: Take 1

(Scene opens with wife approaching husband, who comes in late slamming the door behind him.)

Wife: Where have you been? I was worried about you. You didn't show up for dinner and I began to worry because you didn't call. What's going on?
Husband: Nothing's going on.
Wife: Obviously something is wrong. Do you want to talk about it?
Husband: There's nothing to talk about!
Wife: Well, clearly you are upset. What's going on?

(There is a long pause before husband begins speaking.)

Husband: I'm sick of all of it: work, this boring existence, demanding kids, nothing but problems! I'm sick of it all!
Wife: Do you want to talk about it?
Husband: What is there to talk about? It is what it is!
Wife: I want to help. Is there anything I can do?
Husband: Yeah, just go away and leave me alone.

(Wife is left standing next to the door as husband brushes past her to the study, slamming the door behind him.)

Childish Husband: Take 2

(Scene opens with wife approaching husband, who comes in late slamming the door behind him.)

Wife: Where have you been? You didn't show up for dinner and I began to worry because you didn't call. What's going on?
Husband: I am not a good place right now. Let me decompress a bit. Can we talk later when I have had a chance to calm down?

(A little later, wife finds husband in dining room, resting with head down on his arms.)

Wife: Do you feel comfortable enough now to let me know what's going on?

Husband: It's a lot of things. Work, I'm worried about potential layoffs, our finances, and the long hours I have to work these days.

Wife: I suspected you had a lot on your mind, but why didn't you come to me earlier?

Husband: I was afraid that you would overreact. I could tell that you were becoming a bit standoffish yourself. I feel like you don't care for me anymore when I get the silent treatment.

Wife: I admit that I have been withdrawn lately. I guess I was fearful as well. You have been coming home late and I took that as you had a problem with me.

Husband: I should have come to you days ago. I regret not telling you what was on my mind.

Wife: No apologies necessary. I'm just happy we are talking again! Can we talk more during dinner?

(Husband gets up from chair and hugs wife. They are seen walking peacefully on their way to the kitchen.)

What can be learned from these two scenarios?

The first scenario shows the husband hanging onto resentments without attempting to get to the real causes of the problem. He is unwilling to engage in constructive dialogue and would rather push his wife away. She seems eager and willing to listen and offer support. The fact that he is going it alone sends the signal that he is going to stay in the problem and isolate alone with it. It is possibly a pattern that the husband and the wife have repeated in previous encounters. This habit makes a deeper revelation of underlying issues and solutions unlikely. The longer this kind of interaction is perpetuated, the less likely there will be any improvement in emotional growth.

The second scenario suggests a healthier outcome. Yes, the husband is willing to defer a dialogue until he can approach it with calm. The wife respects her husband's need for a little extra time to calm down but cares enough to reengage. The husband then owns his issues and feelings and has the insight and courage to reveal his feelings. It's clear that there has been a pattern of emotionally mature dialogue. The result suggests that this is a nurturing couple who genuinely care about each other's well-being. Taking time to calm down may be just the thing couples need to do to eventually get to a more rational dialogue.

I have heard that I need to lower my pulse rate. I can count my beats for fifteen seconds and then multiply that number times four. If my pulse rate is above my baseline, I will need to take a break for twenty minutes or so to get a reset on my emotions.

Here are two more scenarios that feature interactions between a boss and direct report. Emotional intelligence principles are often not applied in a work environment, particularly during the heat of battle. A stressful work environment may not always make it easy to practice emotionally intelligent dialogue, particularly when both parties are not in sync or do not desire a rational dialogue.

Angry Boss: Take 1

(Scene opens with angry boss storming into creative director's office.)

Boss: I thought I asked you a week ago for names of writers that we can use on the XYZ project. You knew that we might win the business. Well, we got it! We need to hit the ground running. Where is the list?

Creative director: I'm sorry boss, but you know I've been up to my eyeballs in meeting deadlines for other projects.

Boss: This is what grinds me most. You can't seem to get it through your head that you are a manager. That means you are responsible for having enough staff for the work. I put you in charge of keeping a catalogue of outside vendors and writers we can contact when they are needed. When are you ever going to get with the program?

Creative director: Wait a minute! I have been working twelve-hour days for months now. You told us that we weren't managers but "performance athletes" who would have to stay 100 percent applied on projects. You said that we had to keep expenses down, and if we had to, we should do the creative writing to keep the costs down.

Boss, raising his voice: Hold on. Did I ever say that you should do away with your management tasks? No! You must make better choices on how you will get the work done. When are you going to start behaving like a manager instead of a writer?

Creative director: Don't yell at me. I don't deserve this abuse. I'm doing the best I know how to do. You know all the projects I have on my plate. What projects would you suggest I defer?

Boss: I'm not taking anything off your plate. I expect you to do your job and that includes *everything* I ask you to do!

(Boss slams both hands on desk and leaves office.)

Creative director: I'm calling human resources. I'm not going to take this anymore.

Angry Boss: Take 2

Scene opens with angry boss storming into creative director's office.

Boss: I thought I asked you a week ago for names of writers that we can use on the XYZ project. You knew that we might win the business. Well, we got it! Where is the list?

Creative director: I'm sorry, boss, but you know I've been up to my eyeballs in meeting deadlines for other projects.

Boss: This is what grinds me most. You can't seem to get it through your head that you are the manager in charge of keeping a catalogue of outside vendors and writers we can reach out to when we need to. When are you going to get up to speed?

Creative director: Boss, I did remember you telling me to get that list of outside writers we can use going forward. I apologize for not getting it to you by now. I messed up.

Boss: Yes, you did! We just sold that XYZ project and we're going to have to have a team of writers here now!

Creative director: No excuses. I admit I let that slip. At the time, I didn't want to dangle potential work to writers until I was able to offer something more concrete for them. I didn't want to hire writers until I knew we had a project for them. Let me get started right now. I'll get my lead creative manager to pick up on some of the projects where I'm currently the developer, and I will have a list on your desk by close of business tomorrow. You can approve the ones you want from my recommendations, and I will get the contracts approved for them to start work on Monday.

Boss: All right, but they'd better be good! I want that list of good candidates on my desk tomorrow!

(Boss slams both hands on desk and leaves office.)

Creative director: You will have them tomorrow!

I can identify with the dynamics in play during the first scenario. I have had similar interactions, particularly when the workload is overwhelming and the stress created by deadlines looms large.

Bosses are bosses and they expect their teams to fulfill the demands they make. The first scenario reveals what may be a bossy boss who is not happy with what he sees as a critical assignment that was ignored. The employee is equally pressured having to do the work of a manager and a worker.

They both wonder why the other person can't see the reality of each other's position. What happened though is the dialogue escalated into all out conflict. Emotional intelligence went wanting and was replaced with what each thought was justified anger. Clearly this resulted in even a bigger issue and left the original problem unsolved.

The second scenario revealed at least a willingness on the employee's part to admit when he was wrong. The boss was still angry and disappointed, but the employee was willing to honestly explain his situation without making it an excuse. He then offered a solution that would get the boss what he was asking for. Was the boss a reasonable boss? Maybe not. But the scenario shows that emotional intelligence skills can be practiced even if one of the parties is unaware or unwilling to engage in an emotionally intelligent manner.

Developing Emotional Intelligence Skills

What are the specific areas and opportunities for growing one's emotional intelligence skills? According to Travis Bradberry and Jean Greaves in *Emotional Intelligence 2.0,* there are four areas where growth is possible:

> - self-awareness
> - self-management skills
> - social awareness
> - relationship management skills

For me, personal competence boils down to my ability to behave myself, and social competence is my ability to get along with others. I realize this is an oversimplification; therefore, I encourage you to read the book *Emotional Intelligence 2.0* by Travis Bradberry for additional information.

Without trying to replace the insights offered in the book, I will share reactions from what I learned from reading that book. It is my belief that you shouldn't have to become a psychologist or therapist to be able to behave better, particularly in relationships.

This journey will feature the balance between the part of our brain that regulates logic and emotion. Researchers have said that thoughts emanate from the spinal column and then go through the limbic system, which regulates emotion. These thoughts can then go to the frontal lobe, where logical responses are formed.

I have been told for years that I should get in touch with my feelings. After much therapy, I am working to develop a better emotional vocabulary. I want to better verbalize how I feel at any given moment in time.

I have also been told that I shouldn't let my feelings get the best of me. I was told I should make decisions from a basis of thoughtful consideration, logically weighing alternatives to arrive at the choice(s) that provide the most for what is appropriate for the situation. I have also been told that feelings aren't facts. Clearly this requires balance and discernment if I am to clarify and choose between head or heart alternatives.

I recognize my feelings and want to be sensitive to the feelings of others. This will require more care in selecting words and actions when I am responding to others. If I am more careful prior to interacting, I suspect I will be a happier person and a better friend and associate to those I would help. If I am successful, won't it also enable me to live and let live as well?

I have learned that we all have three distinct qualities: intelligence quotient, emotional quotient, and personality. The only one of these three qualities that we can effectively change is EQ. What can I do to improve my EQ? I can work on four skills: self-awareness, self-management, social awareness, and relationship management skills.

Self-Awareness

When I took my fourth step inventory in Alcoholics Anonymous for the first time, I remember that it was fear that prolonged my decision to start writing my inventory. I had the help of a "brother" from a local Catholic prep school who was patient and loving enough to finally get me to do it. I was afraid because I knew I had done a lot of things that I was unwilling to share with anyone. He put me at ease by sharing his inventory with me, and this gave me the courage to write my own inventory. After I shared my inventory with this generous man, I began to see my tendencies on how I reacted to life events.

Self-awareness requires honesty. For alcoholics like me, it requires rigorous honesty. I must own my part in interactions with other people. Like the Big Book of AA says, "I step on the toes of others, and they retaliate." In the past, I just focused on their retaliation and not in the part I played to cause them to retaliate. Knowing this about some of my tendencies, I must continue to daily evaluate where I have been selfish, dishonest, resentful, and afraid. When agitated, I must pause and ask my Higher Power for the right thought or action. If I honestly look at conflicts I have had with others, wasn't there a behavior on my part that got the ball rolling?

Weren't there key points in a dialogue with others where I may have overreacted and caused an escalation of conflict? I can recall times that may have started as a discussion with a friend about differences in political opinion but dissolved into needless criticism and hurtful attack. If I am self-aware, will I be able to avoid arguments that put relationships at risk?

I can think of a recent occurrence that revealed my lack of self-awareness. I was scrolling through Facebook posts and came across a post that put a politician I did not like in a bad light. The meme suggested that this person may have had political motives that furthered her political desires rather than her concern for the well-being of her constituents. There were numerous reactions to the post, all of them uncomplimentary. I too added my reaction, based on anger toward her actions for which I vehemently disagreed. I called her a "political sellout."

And while most of the people who responded liked my comment, there was one exception. A member of my church reacted with a scathing response. He shared that he thought the language I used was inappropriate. He was extremely disappointed to see these kinds of posts for any political leader, regardless of their party affiliation. He shared that my response did not speak well of the person he knew me to be.

How did I react? I responded with a snarky "Which word did you find most offensive … political or sellout?" This initiated an ongoing stream of defensive posturing that was intended to justify my position. While the interaction cooled down somewhat, what did it accomplish?

I have to say that I find this individual pompous and pious. He is also extremely thoughtful and well informed and perhaps a bit negative and relatively single-minded. He is sort of like me! I don't know what kind of relationship we will have in the future, but had I paused and considered saying something like "political opportunist" rather than "political sellout," the resulting word war might not have occurred. I sincerely regret my actions and am praying that God forgive me for my shortcomings. With God's help, I will not repeat offensive behavior. I have since given myself a time-out from Facebook and will not engage again until I know I can behave the way God wants me to behave.

Self-awareness is not just about being aware of just my defects or negative tendencies. It's also about awareness of all of me—my strengths as well as my weaknesses.

The researchers say that the most successful people have very high self-awareness of all their attributes so they can take full advantage of opportunities.

Self-awareness is foundational to emotional intelligence. If I am not self-aware, I will not be able to grow in the remaining EQ skills.

I have worked with thousands of managers in my career as a consultant, and in hindsight, I can now attest that very few of them had a highly developed sense of self-awareness. There were exceptions.

One of the best managers I have ever worked with was a perfect example of someone who was self-aware. When others around her seemed stressed and even fearful, she was there for all of us as a person unaffected by the stressors of our environment. She never let her emotions get the best of her. She was able to make the transition from emotional to rational appropriately and effectively.

Employees and even other managers often came to her when issues in the workplace seemed to get the best of them. This is not to say that my manager didn't have some of the same feelings that others experienced, but she never let them get in the way of her actions. She always had a cheerful countenance, but she could be firm and decisive even in the face of office turmoil.

The person she reported to was tough and had a bit of a reputation. She could be bubbly and amiable, and if she approved of you, she could be an ally. However, if you got on her bad side, she could make life difficult. She punished anyone who did not meet her expectations. There was rarely a second chance. Many of her direct reports lived in fear, and even though I was an outside consultant working with the group, I avoided her except when working with her directly. There were several employees who had been fired, demoted, ostracized, or transferred because of her. Her judgment was swift and final.

On the other hand, my manager never let fear get in her way of getting the work done. She was highly effective even in the face of conflict. She was aware of her strengths and weaknesses and played to her strengths. She was one of the few persons I have worked with who was able to tolerate the discomfort of working with a difficult boss. If she was afraid of her boss, like the rest of us were, it didn't stop her from consistently interacting with a calm strength. She displayed a quiet courage by not letting fear keep her from doing the next right thing.

Her office door was rarely closed. She welcomed the team to share their concerns. She was available to encourage the rest of us to focus on things we had the power to change.

Self-Management

What I am learning is that self-management isn't about the situational events that are mostly inconsequential, like when I trip over the rug that my wife rolled up to make room for her yoga mat. I may say something like "Is she trying to kill me?" as I pick myself up from the fall. Events like that come and go, but in and of themselves, they may not require much self-management. I need to evaluate my tendencies for when my behavior requires self-management. For me, social media, particularly Facebook, presents opportunities for me to practice self-management.

A couple of days after my Facebook tussle with the member from my church, I came across a meme that said something like "In life, it's important to know when to stop arguing with people and simply let them be wrong."

After numerous two-hundred-word posts trying to bend my nemesis to my way of thinking, I finally sent a post that pretty much communicated the essence of the meme. I thought about unfriending this person but decided that whatever feelings this person exposed, I didn't have to share them. I would stop revealing the exact nature of my faults to everyone who could see my post.

If I reengage with Facebook, when a person shoots a volley over my bow, I can choose to hit one of the emoji responses without any further comment, or I do not have to react at all. I can just keep on scrolling. For me, this is a new tendency, and one that reflects better self-management. This small improvement does not justify any celebration just yet. I can point to the successful moment, but what about consistency of execution over time?

Social Awareness

This is a growth opportunity for most who seek emotional intelligence—not so much in the ability to identify how others may feel in a situation but in the understanding of what is really going on with them.

As an ex-consultant and meeting facilitator, I worked with large groups of managers with diverse backgrounds and interests; these were successful businesspeople with well-formed opinions on topics I presented. I was adept at conference leading and engaging groups to discuss and ultimately to commit to actions they might be willing to take. The company that paid me had expectations as well. This required good listening skills but also the ability to clarify various points of view and the ability to uncover root cause issues that might thwart the possibility of even elementary buy-in. It required me to put my prejudices and biases on the shelf even if I had strong views in favor of my pet actions and solutions. Often I had to be willing to understand what kept them from buying into what I thought were mutually beneficial solutions.

There were times when a company wanted me to work with franchisees to work on their customer retention. I would make a case to show that higher customer retention would not only be good for the company but also for their individual franchises. In my mind, I had the facts on my side. I was able to show attendees that the franchises with the highest customer retention made the most money as well. It sounded good in theory, but I could see that there were attendees who sat there with their arms folded and skeptical looks on their faces. I would ask, "Does anyone have any questions?" Crickets. The easy road would have been to say, "Well, if there aren't any questions, I guess we can move on to the next topic."

I learned that the better way to get to the heart of issues was to surface concerns sooner rather than later. I would say something like "Mr. Smith, I don't want to jump to any false assumptions, but I couldn't help notice that you appeared to have doubts when I showed the relationship between customer retention and profits. Would you be willing to share your concerns?"

Now no matter what that person said, I could use what they said as a springboard to clarify individual motives and include others in the conversation. When I wanted to know the real underlying feelings, it required risks to not only ask tough questions but also be prepared to get answers that weren't always in sync with the goals of the parent company. I always found that dealing with the underlying reality always served the mutual outcomes desired of all parties concerned.

The other thing that I learned during my consultations is that I had to accept the truth regarding individual and smaller group consensus even if it did not always square with what I believed to be true or what the client who was paying me wanted. If I got to underlying causes and conditions, I have found that honest intent for progress is better than phony compliance that lacked commitment.

Relationship Management

If self-awareness is a prerequisite for emotional intelligence, then relationship management is where the rubber hits the road. All healthy relationships require nurturing—a sustained effort to show that a connection is desired and a willingness to put in the work to keep the bond strong. Some relationships just might not warrant the effort, however.

It's during stressful times that relationship management is most at risk. Many find that when the storm clouds appear, what they thought were solid relationships turned out to be nothing but superficial niceties. Fair weather friends abound on the surface but are motivated solely by their underlying currents of the question "What have you done for me lately?"

I have people commit to a visit or an event where they pledged to meet with me, but then, just prior, called or texted to say that something came up and while they really were disappointed that they couldn't make it this time that they would make it up to me real soon. Hey, stuff happens that can't be foreseen, right? But then I found out that the friend in question was seen at another event on the same date and time that they had committed to me. What does this say about the relationship? Does it need to be managed? If it's a not a close relationship, I would probably move on. If it's more than that, some communication may be in order.

Solid relationships require a mutual desire to sustain the bond. Frequent contact, sincere sympathy, empathy, a shoulder to cry on, and demonstration that one cares are vital in relationships that matter. It takes work to consider the needs and wants of others without sacrificing core values. While I really don't want to offend anyone, I find that many people are offended nonetheless. When I proclaim my values, beliefs, and opinions to others, I may unwittingly get an onslaught of value judgment in return.

This is particularly true with social media. If I am honest and have the courage of my convictions, I shouldn't worry about dissenting points of view. I attract folks with similar views and annoy and possibly alienate those who disagree. Relationship management skills should not include kowtowing or being a doormat to anyone who doesn't bring at least a small dose of civility and perhaps skin a little thicker than tissue to an online experience.

On the other hand, emotional maturity is accepting folks the way they are, warts and all. I bring all of me to an interaction whether it's online, virtual, or face-to-face. It's up to me to decide if I choose to invest the work necessary for an authentic relationship. But what about people who do not want to invest in anything authentic? They are part of the relationship management milieu that may require different tactics and skills to interact successfully. I may choose to set boundaries to avoid interactions that may be emotionally harmful or selfish—particularly with people I know who constantly provide the triggers that will set me off. I may be cordial and polite but not engage them beyond casual interaction.

Personal relationships require effort and attention, but what about work relationships? For years, I would hear managers defend their actions as justifiable with the overused epithet "It was nothing personal; it was just business." The implication was business doesn't require relationships to be personal. I have discovered after working with numerous successful companies that their business thrived because of solid relationships internally with their employees and externally with their clients. I have learned that this is just as important for work relationships as personal ones. In fact, it is the core ingredient for turning customers into clients. It makes sense. Companies like JD Power give their highest customer satisfaction scores to companies who work to earn their clients' trust and demonstrate their commitments in a way that exceeds clients' needs. Additionally, they conduct employee satisfaction research to evaluate internal relationships within companies.

Where would most employees rather work? Would they rather work for a company that treats them as an expendable resource that must be controlled? Or would they prefer to work for a company where they are seen as team members to be valued and nurtured? These enlightened companies know that their employees are not expenses to be managed but assets to be cherished and developed. They have found that happy employees attract happy customers. There is a direct correlation between employee satisfaction and client retention. Companies who retain their employees are likely to retain their clients.

My considerations for improving relationship management include

> giving and receiving feedback well
> trusting and being trustworthy
> facing reality
> acting decisively
> communicating decisions and involving stakeholders in choices that impact them
> reserving getting mad for when I am genuinely mad
> not avoiding difficult conversations
> being authentic
> respecting other points of view
> clarifying how others feel
> growing my emotional intelligence

I am learning to keep the pathways clear and navigable between my emotions and my intellect. This requires practice in discernment and choice. Over time, I am developing habits in how I travel between the emotional and logical parts of my brain. Keeping my pathway open and running smoothly will have a large impact on how well I progress with emotional intelligence and my goal to live and let live.

I must become more flexible in choosing how I react. I may start with an emotional reaction, but how long I stay there may impact how well I can get to an effective outcome.

If my cat Domino starts scratching the furniture and my habit reaction is to yell at the cat, I will likely continue to react the same way unless I discard the old behavior and practice a better behavior. My expectation for the cat is to not scratch the furniture. After a while, you would think that I would realize that the cat has got me trained rather than the other way around. I have learned that she does this as a means of getting my attention when I won't play with her. I have gone so far as to sit on the edge of the couch and when the cat approaches to scratch, I start yelling, "No, no, no, no," as I place my arms as an obstacle between the couch and her. The cat thinks this is great fun. This is what she wanted from the beginning. Now she has yet another game that she has taught me to play. For a while, I had a spray bottle next to my chair and when the cat started scratching the couch, I fumbled around trying to find the spray bottle. She figured out that the water was more mist than spray so after a short romp away she returned with her squinty eyes prepared for the game to continue. There I was, squirt bottle in hand, yelling, "No, no, no" to a cat that refused to respond to my verbal commands. My emotional intelligence score so far with this animal was in negative numbers.

My wife observed this comedy and said nothing. She quietly retrieved one of the cat's scratch pads and moved it next to the couch. The cat immediately started scratching the pad instead of the couch while giving me her "I'm more emotionally mature than you" looks.

My wife and I value timeliness on different levels. She doesn't think being a few minutes either side of intended time is that big of a deal. I want to be on time; in fact, I prefer to arrive early. I value punctuality almost to a fault. Let's say we are going to a movie that starts at 7:00 p.m. I would like to be in the car at 6:30 p.m. so that we can get to the movie theater by 6:45 p.m. I remind my wife at 6:25 p.m. that I will be in the car and ready to leave in five minutes. It seems that that there is always "one more thing" for my wife to do before she is ready to leave. More likely than not, I am in the car at 6:30 p.m. banging my fists on the steering wheel and honking the horn in disgust as she is still in the process of doing her "one more thing." My emotional brain is in hyperdrive! Reading this, I can see that I get exercised over what is likely a trifle. I admit that I have not navigated the pathway from emotional to logical successfully for these interactions. I keep falling for the self-imposed emotional trap of "Doesn't she know how important it is to be on time?" I must remember from behavior modification training principles that everyone's behavior makes sense to them.

Looking logically at these repetitive "time plays" suggests there is a need to respond better. Next time, I am not going to stay in the inevitable frustration mode. I am going to accept the times when she misses my time expectation with the thought that this is just how she rolls. Rather than raise my voice and honk the horn, I will proceed without any admonition. However, every time she does make it at the time I requested, I intend on saying something like "Thank you for respecting my preference to leave a little early." But why can't I think of these alternatives in the heat of the moment? Clearly, I will need to replace my bad habit with a better one.

Emotional intelligence lends a new perspective on how I think. The takeaway for me is my desire now to pause and reflect when the emotions start to occupy my brain negatively. The adage of just slowly counting to ten when provoked makes even more sense now that I am aware of how my brain works. I also believe, however, that once I get to thinking rather than emoting it would be helpful to be able to draw upon skills and approaches that permit consistent success. What are these new and better habits going to look like?

When I am confronted with a situation that has me riled or in some other emotion that has me stymied, what will I do? I will pause sufficiently to get into my thinking brain. I will direct thoughts that will enable a more centered rather than a scattered solution. Are there words to use and approaches to take that will aid my ability to relate with others? Perhaps. If I find them and use them, will it aid my quest for emotional integrity and maturity? If yes, then improving my communication skills may be at the top of the list.

5

Communication Skill

Communication Basics

Many people suffer from the delusion that they have actually communicated. Everyone desires to understand and to be understood, so a review of the basics of communication might be helpful.

Communication is the process of transmitting information, beliefs, attitudes, and ideas from one person to another. It takes many forms: verbal, written, nonverbal, and visual. Relational growth cannot take place without effective communication between individuals. How well we communicate is likely the single most important ingredient in successful relationships. Is it science? Is it an art? It is both.

Let's look at the mechanics of verbal communication. It requires a sender and a receiver. If I am talking to another person, I must assure that they can hear me. Am I speaking loudly enough and clearly enough for them to discern the words? Do the sounds I am emitting reach the ear canal of the person to whom I am communicating? If yes, then on a basic level I know I am being heard. I can confirm by asking, "Can you hear me?" If I get an affirmative, I know that I have been heard.

That is only the first part of the verbal communication process. The real question that needs to be answered is "Am I being understood?" That of course requires more than just hearing but listening. Listening requires focus and interaction to assure comprehension. Skillful interaction assures that the intended message sent is the one that is received. Who is ultimately responsible for assuring that the message sent is the same as the one received? While success of the outcome of communication requires effort by both the speaker and the listener, the burden of responsibility for good communication always belongs with the speaker or sender.

Effective communication also assumes there is a willingness on the part of the listener to care enough to connect. Of course, there are many other variables to avoid miscommunication and misunderstanding. Here is an illustration.

There was a young woman who was preparing to go on her first date with a young man she really liked. With her mom's help, she selected a beautiful dress, and it was perfect in every way except the girl, upon inspection in the mirror, thought that she might look a bit more mature if she enhanced the bodice. She found some socks and discovered if she strategically placed them in her dress, the look she was going for made her appear a bit more developed. Just before the young man arrived, she asked her mom how she looked. Her mom was delighted, but after a short pause, she suggested that there might be one more thing that would complete the ensemble. She went to her bedroom and returned with a pearl necklace. The girl was overwhelmed. Just as Mom finished helping with the necklace, the doorbell rang. The door was opened, and there was the young man appearing well scrubbed but extremely nervous.

The date went as well as two young people who were dating for the first time could want. And as the young man returned the girl to the front door to say goodbye, he took the girl's hands, looked into her eyes, and nervously asked, "Are those real?" The girl dissolved into tears and ran inside, leaving the confused young man to wonder what had happened. The boy was referring to the pearls, and the girl incorrectly thought the boy had caught on to her padding ruse.

This illustration points out just how some communication can lead to misunderstanding and unintended consequences. Unfortunately, what we say doesn't always communicate what we intend.

I expect it will require learning and practicing skills that will improve the likelihood of my communication success. I will start by choosing words more carefully. Words have power to affect attitude and perhaps even a person's physical health. I have heard that words drive behavior. Repeated behaviors become habits. Repeated habits define character. I pledge to develop better communication habits.

Communicating More Effectively

There are numerous suggestions on how to improve communication skills. Just Google the topic and see how many you will find. I have discovered that the skills needed for sustaining relationships often are repeated in the suggestions for good communication. The skills are interdependent. I have been working to improve my communication skills for my entire lifetime. I believe I have made some progress toward my goal, but I have a long way to go. Here are the elements of communication I am working to improve.

Listening. I can't listen if I can't hear. I have a rather profound hearing loss. I wear hearing aids to mitigate the condition. Anyone who depends on them knows they do not help as much as glasses do to improve vision. I have learned to read lips to a certain extent, but the inability to hear parts of key conversations is an obstacle. When COVID-19 restrictions required mask wearing, it became even more troublesome. If the conversation is important, then I must find the best possible environment to assure reception. Even when the conditions are ideal, my responses to what I thought I heard are sometimes humorous. Many of my hearing miscues are unfortunately age related.

I saw a greeting card recently that showed a distinguished couple in formal attire. The woman was leaning back into the man's embrace and said, "And if I tilt my head just so, darling, there is less screech from our hearing aids."

Other times, it can be embarrassing and even problematic. I empathize with others with hearing loss and listen to them struggle to connect with repeated questions of "What? What? What hat did you say?" I can relate to the following story.

An old man was wondering if his wife had a hearing problem. One night, he stood behind her while she was sitting in her lounge chair. He spoke softly to her. "Honey, can you hear me?" There was no response. He moved a little closer and said again, "Honey, can you hear me?" Still, there was no response. Finally, he moved right behind her and said directly into her ear, "Honey, can you hear me?" She replied, "For the third time, yes!"

Sadly, it isn't that funny. Eventually, those who hear normally lose patience and either end the conversation or exaggerate their volume to make themselves heard. Dialogues require the ability to hear. If you are unable to hear you can't listen. If you don't listen, you will not understand. *Merriam-Webster's Collegiate Dictionary* defines hearing as "the process, function, or power of perceiving sound; specifically: the special sense by which noises and tones are received as stimuli." Listening, on the other hand, means "to pay attention to sound; to hear something with thoughtful attention; and to give consideration." Hearing is physiological, but listening also has a psychological element. Good communication requires both hearing and listening, but to grow emotionally and relationally, my focus will be on listening. Good listening assumes that both parties want to engage, and that requires respect for the person who initiates the conversation. You can tell when someone is not listening.

I am guilty of not paying attention. Sometimes my mind wanders too much. Recently during a lengthy discourse, my wife stopped midsentence and asked, "Have you been listening?" What followed on my part ended poorly as I responded with a childish yes. She asked, "Then what did I say?" I mumbled something that wasn't even close to what she had said and got the rebuke I deserved.

I must learn to focus and seek to understand what my friend or spouse says if I ever hope to communicate effectively. Do I really listen, or am I just waiting to hammer home my point of view? Am I preoccupied or distracted? Am I just going through the motions when listening? Am I genuinely engaged? Am I willing and able to clarify what I heard? Am I willing to repeat what I heard being said and ask additional questions to be sure I understand? Do I keep my emotions in check and remain objective with my responses?

I not only have to focus when there is a direct dialogue but be diligent when I communicate using other media, particularly text or email. Texting is an opportunity to pay close attention and take the time when reading and responding to be sure my intent and delivery are successful. I need to take the time to read carefully, checking for intent before I hit send.

I have learned through many years of working as a consultant that the quality of communication is the responsibility of the sender. When I send texts or am talking voice-to-voice, I must assure that my communication is clear, respectful, and considerate. I can accomplish being respectful and considerate by answering these three questions in the affirmative.

> - Is it kind?
> - Is it true?
> - Is it necessary?

Social media has proved challenging for me. I must admit that I have not always been willing to take the high road. Am I willing to just keep scrolling when I find antagonistic content? Do I get carried away with the passion of my positions? Am I consciously or unconsciously provoking those who will read my posts? I do not need to respond to every meme I see. I can consciously choose to avoid friction.

Bottom line is I must be willing to listen. It must show. My body language should include good eye contact and facial expressions that show attention and respect. The goal of good communication is understanding. Did my listener end up understanding what I said? And if the responsibility for understanding falls with the me, how do I know for sure that the message was understood?

My job required a lot of communication with clients. I learned over time that a person can talk too much. I have talked my way out of a sale—and sometimes out of getting work. I have the two ears and one mouth, which suggests I need to listen twice as much as I talk. I recently came across an acronym that I need to remember: WAIT, which means "Why am I talking?" Thinking before speaking keeps me from putting my foot in my mouth. Those times when I have said something without thinking about the consequence are the times that I wished I would have paused a bit and prayed for guidance. The

Holy Spirit is here to guide me. If I wait for the Spirit to guide me, I am better off.

Effective understanding requires a listener to be engaged. I've heard the process called "active listening." What makes the listening active? It is the effort extended by the listener to understand what the speaker is communicating. It may require the listener to pause the dialogue to check in with what they have heard. They can say something like "Let me see if understand what you have said so far. I heard you to say _____ [recounting what was heard]. Am I on track with what you intended?" This back-and-forth clarification leads both parties to have a mutual understanding. The parties may not believe in or agree with the message, but they will at a minimum understand what was communicated. Above all, I strive to listen to others without placing value. I need to remain neutral, and if my emotion starts to override my rational interpretation, I will pause and refocus.

Civility. I have a friend who is known for his blunt and sometimes off-putting responses in the name of being totally honest. When he gets caught up in the emotion from his heartfelt passion, he often resorts to name-calling and position bashing. He was told by his sponsor, "Anything that can be said can be said nicely." While he has not always conformed to his sponsor's suggestion, he has lowered the volume by a few decibels. Does this show progress on his part? He is growing spiritually, which is reducing the number of outbursts. The truth lies partially in his improvement and perhaps as much in those who know him becoming more tolerant.

The need for civility is particularly noticeable in social media. Perhaps it's the supposed anonymity that emboldens us. When someone posts a meme or shares a comment that ruffles, the hand grenades start to fly. Is it possible to communicate an opposing point of view without denigrating the intended audience? Yes, and I pledge to do better in that regard. Texting often has its own inherent challenges, particularly when we are intending something harmless. Without the facial expressions or other body language present during face-to-face dialogue, the message may be misconstrued. My use of humor or personality traits that get me by in person will rarely work if I am on the phone. Some of the humor that may be acceptable face-to-face may not translate as well via text. It sometimes becomes hurtful rather than humorous.

When the topics are opinion driven, it seems that the communication can get nasty if there is polarity of opinion. It typically is more apparent during presidential elections. People take sides. Red versus blue. Conservative versus liberal. During the last election, I heard some say, "Support sanctuary cities," and others say, "Build a wall." The dialogue between the two sides became divisive. Communication was lost for the passion for the position. I am not without fault. I have had failures in the civility department.

In a recent dustup on Facebook, I ended up feuding with a member of my church, my pastor at the time, and the previous pastor of my church. I was convinced I was right, but because I was so rigid in defense of my position, I likely paid the price with individuals who I did not wish to alienate. Was there a better way to dialogue than the one I chose? Is it possible to stand up for a position without alienating those who have different positions? Yes, but it must start with me. I can choose to be civil. I can take a breath and pause when agitated. I can keep on scrolling when I stumble across a social media post that bugs me.

When I am conversing, I can keep an even tone and not raise my voice. The friend referenced earlier is brilliant and gives his positions considerable weight supported by depth of his understanding that he buoys with numerous facts. He just has one volume: loud. He starts with loud and then crescendos to louder. I have taken the time to learn to love him volume and all. Civility, I believe, is the responsibility of the listener. I can let my friend rant. I choose to value the message more than how it's delivered. If it starts to wear, I just lower the speaker volume on my computer, phone, or hearing aids. Or if it is written text or posts, I can lower the temperature with my word choices. Or I do not have to respond at all. When talking by phone, if I have had enough for one session, I just say I must go, and I leave. Again, the power rests with the listener. I do not have to let a discussion dissolve into angry words.

Respect. Respect is demonstrable, and the only way it can be evaluated is from the perspective of the listener. This is not about intention but about the impact of what is heard and understood. There must be evidence to support any intention to be respectful. After a crime, perpetrators often say they never intended to do any harm. Their intention does not make them any less guilty.

This makes me think of what happens during a service repair call. Before I am connected, I am asked if I would be willing to stay on the line to answer a few questions. Then after the call, there will be computer-generated questions that describe the quality of my experience, and I am then prompted to leave a numerical grade. I wonder what score my listeners might give me if they were asked to complete a survey on how respectful I was. They would have to respond to something like this: "Given a range of one through ten, with ten being the highest, what score would you give to describe the level of respect given to you by the person with whom you just communicated?" For me, that highest level of respect must be earned. I want to demonstrate the highest level of respect during all forms of communication, so what can I do to earn it?

Respect for the listener should start with how their time is valued. If I am talking directly, I should check to see if this is a good time to talk and if they have enough time to talk. The evidence of that respect for time should include sensitivity to the content of what I communicate. Is it concise? Do I avoid idle chatter? If time is an issue, do I check periodically to see how I am doing on time?

How I react to persons whose opinions differ from mine will reflect my level of respect. When engaged in any form of communication, the differences of opinion expressed should never adversely affect respect for the individual or their right to their ideas. My old attempts at humor were not very respectful. When I didn't agree with someone, I might have said something like "I could agree with what you are saying, but then we would both be wrong." Funny? Not funny? As a friend often says, it's the duality of funny.

It is easier to be respectful around friends and family, but what about the chats and texts with persons with whom I do not have any ties? Perhaps it is then even more important to maintain a philosophy of respect. It is not necessary to agree with a position, but it is essential that I treat the person with respect. I have learned the hard way that what I say can and will be used against me in more than just a court of law. My character and value system are in play every time I post, write, or share in person. It comes down to basic decency and respect for everyone. After all, how do I want to be treated? I want to be valued and to know that I matter.

Respect also requires being true to oneself. I shouldn't have to betray a core belief or avoid sharing a long-held opinion in fear of a lack of acceptance. True respect means caring about someone enough to bring my true authentic self to the relationship. Flattery is often insincere. I say the things I think I should say rather than thoughtfully say the things I really mean. I don't want to sink to insincere compliments or throwaway chitchat under the guise of caring. At the same time, I shouldn't brutalize the other person with such blunt honesty that it harms them or others.

Respect also includes a sincere attempt to avoid degradation or undue criticism. In the spirit of total honesty and the courage of my convictions, I have offered unwelcomed admonitions to those I would convert to my way of thinking. Any dialogue on my part starting with the phrase "You should ..." elicits more contempt than respect. Even if I do not agree with the person, I can use something like "I respect your position and your right to have it."

Nonverbal cues. Body language sometimes reveals more than words regarding true feelings when we are engaged in dialogue with another person. While I don't read as much into body language as some, I will check for obvious reactions to what I am saying. Why wouldn't I want to notice gestures and body language if it could improve the quality of my understanding and the quality of the relationships I value?

When talking in person or during a video chat, it is easy to see how facial expressions and body position, or movement, can help to assess effectiveness. On the other hand, if I am texting or posting online, I do not have any of my expressions or gestures to support my intent. The only things I must convey my personality and emotions with are my word choices and emojis. This has been problematic. A missing comma or all caps can send an unintended message, and the recipient(s) may jump to the wrong conclusion because they missed the attempt at humor or tongue-in-cheek sarcasm. In the middle of a pandemic like the one I experienced, this lack of body language required me to be doubly careful before I hit send. The other caution for me is to not interpret what I see in the body language of others without confirmation. If I see someone glancing skyward and to the right or left when they are sharing, it may not mean they are lying. It may just mean they are diverting their attention for a moment. I have been accused in the past of going too far into surfacing the underlying meaning in things my friends say. I shouldn't misinterpret further by adding body language assumptions to what I think others might mean.

Choose the best method. Over time, I have come to rely on texting over voice-to-voice calls. When I was working as a consultant, I learned that my clients would rarely pick up the phone to answer a call, but they might respond with text because it was not as invasive. If they were in a meeting, they might be able to shoot off a quick text to provide an answer or provide direction. The challenge with texting is that there is a total reliance on the written word to offer detail. Texting also lacks the emotional element that face-to-face or voice-to-voice can provide. Texting is useful for permitting reference points for recollection of deadlines or commitments.

For longer and more detailed communication, emails are an option. Like texts, they do not provide any of the additional cues that voice inflection and body language can add to understanding, but they enable a less intrusive interaction. Yet texting and messaging seem to be more and more prevalent even when face-to-face options are available. A while back while I was waiting to conduct a session at an airport hotel venue, I saw two young attendees sitting side by side who appeared to be playing a video game of some sort. I recognized them from previous sessions we had attended. I approached them to find out what had them so enthralled. They informed me they were texting. That wasn't alarming, but then they shared that they were texting each other. Sitting side by side, they preferred to chat via text than to chat face-to-face.

During the COVID-19 pandemic, most of my contact with the outside world was done via Zoom, a video chat app. I am a bit concerned that some of the actions like mandated social distancing, face masks that hide facial expressions, and a lack of physical contact evolve from the "new normal" to permanent policy. Are we to rely less on face-to-face dialogue and rely more on less virtual methods of communication? What does this hold for the future? Will personal and societal relationships become less engaging? I hope not.

Face-to-face communication, either in person or video chat, permits the highest level of engagement. More of the senses can be brought to bear and more of the personalities and emotions of the sender and receiver can be considered during interactions. Voice-to-voice and in person dialogue are the best forms of communication when the relational outcome is most important. Experts say that events like asking someone to marry or breaking up with a long-term relationship require a face-to-face dialogue. Similarly, asking your boss for a raise should not be done via text or email. Choosing the right communication method is important, and honing the skills for each method is essential for establishing and growing relationships.

Personal Communication Challenges

There are numerous challenges to effective communication that can get in the way of my willingness and ability to live and let live.

Need to be right. More and more, people seem to have ironclad opinions of how things should be. This goes well beyond healthy debate where individuals offer their observations and beliefs and then listen to an opposing point of view. It seems that people have made their minds up and there will be no further need for investigation. Any opposing view is met with defensiveness and the feeling of being attacked. The outcome of these closed-minded stances can result in friends being unfriended on social media and—even worse—social media accounts being blocked based on views that are thought to be offensive. It is an era of fact-checkers and thought police. Cancel culture and angry mobs are burning books and tearing down statues. The message is "You will conform to our views or you will be found out and punished." Friends and families are being torn apart and made to choose a side.

Keeping an open mind seems to be a lost art today. I recall my mother asking me, "Would you rather be right or happy?" I would like to be happy, but if I must sacrifice being right, I'm not so sure. So "being right" leads me to join coalitions of others who share a prescribed version of being right. Social media offers groups for me to join, and membership often is approved based on leading questions that prove my unwavering allegiance. Once in the group, we offer stories and observations of life events that support our collective views. We are right and they are wrong. The danger of this rigidity seems self-evident, yet this single-minded fervor continues to flourish over working for unification. No wonder our country suffers from such polarity and divisiveness. Relational growth and civility suffer in favor of self-righteous like-mindedness.

Codependency. The need to seek relationships with others is completely right and normal. If I feel good about myself, it is only natural that I would want to connect with others and share in the vibrancy and love that can come from relating with others. There wouldn't be society without this natural tendency to want to include others. But for addicts like me, there is a tendency to want to go further with my natural instincts. I am like normal people only more so.

Allowing for individual differences and accepting them without judgement are good hallmarks of a healthy relationship. Ideally, I should be able to feel good about my identity and those traits that represent my views while at the same time being able to respect the right of a partner to have their own set of needs and values. That sense of independence requires a healthy sense of self.

The ability to allow another person to be themselves for who they are based on their individual views is important. At the same time, I shouldn't feel the need to sacrifice my values and my truth to get along with others.

Having read some of the descriptions of codependency, I was surprised to find that I share some of the symptoms. I still occasionally suffer from the delusion that I am responsible for my wife's happiness. Like they say, "Happy wife, happy life." And while I desire my wife to be happy, I know at least intellectually that I can't make anyone else happy. Happiness is an inside job. Yet I let my wife's moods affect my own, particularly when she is down and feeling depressed. I still have a lot of room for growth to be able to detach sufficiently and not fall into step with her moods, particularly when she's unhappy.

Another characteristic for my codependency is my tendency to give up my life decisions to someone who disagrees with them. I wanted to move to Florida, but a friend told me that it would be a bad place to go. I must admit I let that person's opinion of my decision have more influence than it deserved. Another behavior that might be considered codependent is to go along with someone's choice just to avoid conflict. Whenever I have done that in the past, I end up feeling hurt or resentful with the additional pain of discovering it was never that important to the other person.

Sadly, I must admit that I spend an inordinate amount of time trying to change my spouse. My wife and I have differing opinions on the importance of timeliness. She is not as driven by the need to be on time. I on the other hand have a strong desire to not be late but also to show up early. I have discovered that this is just another form of codependence. I need her to do what I want her to do. History shows that I do not have a healthy enough sense of self to allow her to value timeliness the way she prefers. I vacillate between resentment for her tardiness and finding a way of not letting her preference become my problem. A while back, we agreed to a compromise that permitted me to drive separately if she wasn't ready. Why did my attitude toward accepting that compromise slip away? Why do I go back to the habit of thinking she will change? The simple explanation is that I am still codependent.

Use of humor. I react with humor as a way of dealing with stress and to lighten the burden of daily living. Insensitivity to other people when trying to be funny sometimes alienates them and leads to outcomes that are anything but humorous. There is often a tiny line between sharp wit and cruel sarcasm. Regretfully, there are times I use humor at the expense of individuals' feelings. If my attempts at humor are falling short, what am I to do? One tact is to tell the listeners to lighten up and quit taking things so seriously. Another more appropriate reaction is to read the room and apologize for any offense. Again, the decision as to whether it was funny or just crude or insensitive is up to the audience.

And while self-directed humor through self-deprecation may be good for humility, it can often backfire if the audience ends up piling on instead of laughing it off. If I am to use self-deprecating humor, I had better develop a bit of thick skin so that I do not fall prey to my childish tendency to be overly sensitive. That may lead to another obstacle to communication: defensiveness.

Defensiveness. When people accused me of being defensive, I argued that there was a difference between being defensive and defending a strongly held point of view. When I was accused of being defensive, I admit to saying something like "The reason I am so defensive is that you are so offensive."

So much for my rationalizations. What is defensiveness, and how might it become detrimental to relational communication? How do I know if I have a tendency for defensiveness? Here are some signs:

> I may throw colleagues under the bus to deflect blame from myself.
> I come up with trivial excuses for poor results.
> I use flippant remarks to deflect or minimize criticism.
> I pout or sit in silent scorn with arms folded and legs crossed.
> I interrupt with an attack of those who are offering criticism.
> I do not listen but counterattack with numerous reasons why criticism is unwarranted.
> My face turns red and my pulse elevates when I get feedback.
> I use sarcasm or laugh to minimize impact of those offering feedback.

My AA program suggests that my defensiveness stems from fear. My fear of criticism or lack of approval leads me to respond with many of the behaviors listed above. I now know that defensiveness may also be a result of low emotional intelligence (EQ). I remain in my emotional brain when I react to criticism or information I might think is threatening. I need to transition to my rational brain and react more maturely to criticism. Based on what I am learning, this is no longer a "knowing" problem for me but a "doing" problem. Because of my history of defensiveness, I have been slow to learn and even slower to act.

In a former job, I had responsibility for the development and creation of training materials to be delivered for a broad spectrum of automotive dealership personnel. It was part of launching a new vehicle automotive division and there was a lot at stake. There were numerous members of my team, including me, who had to fulfill various parts of the curriculum.

There were internal reviews and edits, but the real test came when the client had their turn for feedback on what had been developed. I knew prior to the review meeting that there were portions of the materials that would not meet client scrutiny, but ready or not, the content was submitted. The day of reckoning arrived. I knew there would be significant criticism and thought I was prepared emotionally. I was not. I was unable to accept negative feedback on the content developed by members of my team. I became defensive. They were telling me that my baby was ugly. A more emotionally mature manager would have accepted the predictable boos, but when the critique turned to full-on harangue, my fight-or-flight instincts emerged. The child in me cowered, and the defensive adult in me took it all personally. It was a painful process and one that I could have avoided if I had been even-tempered and less defensive. All is well that ends well and the final product was well received. However, if I would have applied what I now know about emotional intelligence and communication skill, I could have avoided some of the suffering.

There are coins people give each other in AA that have writing on both sides. One side says, "Rule 62." The other side states, "Don't take yourself so seriously!" I have received several of these coins over the years from friends who apparently felt I would benefit from this advice. Sometimes these AA friends have mouthed the words "Rule 62" across from me during one of my "I'm a victim" shares. I think I had better start carrying that coin to remind myself to become less defensive.

It's Personal

Until now, I have focused on keys to success and challenges that must be overcome to permit and sustain the ability to communicate on a relational level.

Relationships are sticky and sometimes messy. Stay in one long enough and there will be a time when the going gets tough and the ability to navigate through difficult patches without permanent damage will require focus and all the emotional intelligence a person can muster. These difficult conversations sometimes start innocently enough but can grow into major conflict if they are not treated honestly and thoroughly. The longer it takes to identify and treat the obstacles, the harder it will be to reconcile and restore. I have found that the accumulation of these small and seemingly innocent failures to resolve can have lasting impact on a relationship. Here are a couple of recent events that illustrate the dilemma.

The lease on my wife's car was close to maturation, so we started the process to shop for a replacement. I was a retail operations consultant for automotive dealerships, so I considered myself quite capable of locating a suitable replacement. One key point to remember: this was *going to be my wife's car*. That key fact might have been something I should have kept as priority number one as I launched my search.

My wife's vehicle was a Toyota RAV4 Hybrid. She absolutely loved this SUV. It was loaded with most of the luxury features available and she enjoyed driving it. The simple solution would have been to go back to the Toyota dealership with whom she had a good service experience and lease another Toyota RAV4 Hybrid. There were some additional capabilities that were missing in the RAV4. Since we envisioned moving to Arizona sometime that year, I thought that the ability to tow my motorcycles would not only help with the move but also enable us to tow the motorcycles on vacations. I discovered that Toyota vehicles that were capable of towing were out of our price range. I had worked for GM for several years and was eligible for an employee purchase discount on any GM make. I identified the Chevrolet Blazer as an SUV that also had a towing package available. I recall showing a photo of the vehicle to my wife and telling her the monthly payment. She advised that the lease payment would be around $80 a month higher than our current payment. Taking that as the only objection she had to the purchase, I told the salesperson that I would like to configure payments based on 12,000 miles a year, which would lower the monthly payments. I shared the payment information with my wife and told her that that was the best I could do based on how the lease was configured but failed to tell her the 12,000 miles/year mileage limitation.

We showed up at the dealership to take delivery. My wife had not driven the vehicle and fortunately after the drive she said she liked it. We were then invited into what looked to be a garage area of the dealership that was converted to permit social distancing in addition to masks and gloves required for protection against the COVID-19 virus pandemic.

In the process of reviewing the paperwork, the salesperson recounted the mileage limitations for our lease. My wife heard the 12,000-mile limitation number and that immediately interrupted the proceedings. She said she would need at least a 15,000-mile-per-year limit. Well now, the payment would go up even further. My plan to limit the amount due at signing to a minimum was increased by $1500 to reduce the monthly payments, which although still over budget was closer to acceptable to my wife. Despite raised eyebrows by my wife, we left with the car, and after driving the car home, she said she really liked it. *Whew. I'm out of the woods.*

Not so fast.

I asked my wife afterwards for any examples where failure to communicate might have affected our relationship. She gave a couple of references and then shared, "Yeah, my new car has a cloth interior, and I wanted a leather interior like I had in my Toyota." I had eliminated that option due to price and reasoned that if we moved to Arizona, a leather interior would not be as comfortable in the heat. When I shared the reasoning to my wife, she gave me "the look." It was the "There you go again thinking of yourself" look. In the scheme of things, the car lease experience wasn't that damaging. What did it reveal? I made a decision that affected my wife without thoroughly including her in the process.

We live in Michigan. It goes without saying that the winters here are colder and seem to last longer every year. A couple of years back, I decided to explore alternatives to wintering in Michigan. I knew that many of my friends had already found a way to go south for the winter, and for Michiganders at least, Florida seemed to be the destination of choice. My wife and I traveled to Marco Island one January and found that while the temperature was warmer, the location wasn't to our liking. I had heard about a place called The Villages and decided to take a trip. It was a special introductory offer and I signed us up for a week. My wife didn't like the idea as her prior visits confirmed that this was not a location she cared for that much. I asked if she had a problem with me going and she said it would be OK. I went and loved the place. It was quite congested, but here were a bunch of older people my age who seemed to love the lifestyle. I investigated costs of housing and found them to be within our budget. I was sure that with all the photos I had sent back to report on my newfound wintering solution that my wife would at least reconsider. I returned to Michigan with bounding enthusiasm and was sure that this would be a solution she would love. After all there were hundreds of clubs and organizations and I had checked off all the boxes for the ones that my wife would enjoy. At least I thought I had found the keys to her change of heart. I was wrong. She was not the slightest bit interested in going anywhere in Florida to live. One more time I let my personal choice override a decision that required my wife's needs and preferences.

I asked her if there was anywhere in the country where warmer months of winter might be acceptable. I mentioned that a mutual friend's parents were moving to South Carolina to a place called Margaritaville. We decided to look and drove to Hilton Head Island. We discovered that the fifty-five-plus community we wanted to scope out wasn't that far away. Thank goodness it was unseasonably warm, and we enjoyed the beachy vibe and laid-back ambiance. We made an appointment to visit the community we had heard about. The model homes were phenomenal and seemed to be in reach financially. I was shocked because my wife said she could be happy living here. Wonderful! We finally discovered a solution we could both live with, literally! We told the Realtor that we were interested and would be getting back to her shortly with an answer. During the last several days while we were there, we asked numerous residents what it was like to live there. Almost unanimously they all said they loved it there except for the bugs. They seemed to define each of the seasons not so much with weather patterns but with the type of bugs that arrived for each month of the year. Now it was clear why so many of the homes had such giant screened-in patios. They called them lanais, but they looked like giant cages, and apparently if you never left your cage, the bugs introduce themselves in a way you would not want them to repeat. Neither one of us liked the thought of that many bugs, nor any of the solutions that would permit us to coexist with them. This was a turning point in our search because we agreed to make the decision together and because we both let our rational brains work.

I recall that I heard her say that she liked the desert and had enjoyed our trips to Arizona. Hmmmm. I loved the desert! My wife had a convention in Phoenix, Arizona, and so the month of February would be spent in sunny Phoenix. I went early and my wife joined me for the last half of the month. It was magic. We had a great time, and my wife was OK with the decision to look at homes in fifty-five communities. I had given the Realtor the list of must-haves that my wife would require, and we visited numerous locations in Maricopa County. There were numerous options, and we really liked a couple of them. We both were excited about the prospects of moving. In fact, we had an appointment to meet with the Realtor and put down a deposit. Gratefully, that decision was deferred as we both woke up on the day of the appointment with a sinking feeling caused by what we would do if we could not sell our current home.

Prudence won out that day. We called the Realtor to tell her that we had decided to sell our home in Michigan and return to Arizona with cash in hand. I am convinced today that the thought to postpone was divinely inspired. It was just a short time later that the COVID-19 pandemic left us sheltering in place at our home in Michigan. I can only imagine the panic if we had ended up with a mortgage payment on a new home that we could not occupy. Thank You, God! The Holy Spirit intervened on our behalf!

But wait. There was more to be learned.

On Mother's Day, my son and his wife came to our home to celebrate. We had a great time reconnecting and commiserating over the events that had befallen us. My daughter-in-law inquired as to our plans for the sale of our home and the progress of our move to Arizona. I said that the plans had been suspended but we would proceed in earnest once the virus had been suppressed sufficient to reengage.

My wife must have given a look that betrayed that intention. My daughter-in-law noticed and asked my wife what was on her mind. I was surprised to hear that my wife was having second thoughts about the move. I was shocked as she shared that she did not want to leave her friends and all her activities she had enjoyed in Michigan. My son was as surprised as I was and recalled that we had never sounded happier when we had first announced our intentions. My daughter-in-law responded, "Shouldn't your wife be able to change her mind?"

I didn't bring up the subject for a couple of days, but I finally told my wife how disappointed I was. I thought we had agreed on the move. My wife admitted that she was once excited about the move but that she had fallen back into a routine she really enjoyed in Michigan. I admitted that the move would be a strain on us both but whimpered that all the work we had done in getting our home ready for sale would be for naught. My wife recanted and said that she would keep her original commitment, and I felt relieved for the moment. I knew on some level that my wife was not entirely onboard. I vacillated between mild resentment and resignation as I considered her concerns. If we had used a better communication process, could it have alleviated our differences and enabled us to stay in sync?

Clearly there is no panacea when it comes to spousal communication. As I reflected on the car-buying episode and our "move or stay" decision, I recalled a decision-making process I learned years ago that might provide some direction. It was developed by Kepner/Tregoe to aid decision-making and problem analysis. I used to teach it years ago when I worked for an automotive manufacturer. I recall steps of that process recall that might have saved us some grief if they had been applied.

1. Prior to developing alternatives for the decision, list the things that each alternative must have to be considered.

2. After all parties involved in the decision have agreed on what each alternative must have, generate a list of what you would like to have for each alternative.

3. Generate a list of alternatives for the decision you want to make.

4. Evaluate each alternative against the things that you must have from the decision.

5. Eliminate any of the alternatives that do not meet the must-have criteria.

6. For each of the remaining alternatives, have decision-makers agree on how much each alternative would meet the criteria for each of the like-to-have criteria. (Score each item with one being the least and ten being the most.)

7. Add all the scores for each alternative and the alternative that has passed all the must-haves and then the highest total number for all of the like-to-haves is the likely choice for the decision.

I have used this process in the past when I had to make career move decisions, and while it isn't ironclad, it lends objectivity to decisions that otherwise would be influenced largely on emotion. If all parties affected by the decision complete the process together, the final decision may be more mutually acceptable. The only caveat is to agree on the scores needed for each of the like-to-haves for each alternative. It is also possible overstate the valuation for each of the like-to-haves in favor of a pet alternative.

Decision Matrix for Staying Warm in Winter

Must-Haves (Go or No Go)	1.	2.	3.
warm in winter	go	go	go
affordability	go	go	go
Nice-to-Haves			
property taxes	4	7	6
insurance (house and auto)	4	7	6
HOA expense	3	8	4
maintenance expense	2	7	1
retirement community	4	10	3
moving expense	4	4	10
destination pluses	3	5	9
convenience	5	4	9
new home	0	10	6
selling/buying expense	2	2	9
avoid moving hassle	2	2	10
total	33	66	73

Alternatives

1. Stay in home and buy a second property somewhere warm.
2. Move to Arizona and spend three months in Michigan.
3. Remodel home and spend three winter months somewhere warm.

We chose option 3. We remodeled our home and decided to enjoy at least one winter in Arizona.

Difficult Conversations

The movie *Cool Hand Luke* featured a memorable quote by the antagonist to Paul Newman when he said, "What we've got here is a failure to communicate." Failed crucial conversations are the bane of relationships. The list of challenging and sometimes difficult conversations can include things like the following:

> - asking for someone's hand in marriage
> - asking for a divorce
> - asking for a raise
> - confronting a family member about their drug addiction
> - discussing problems with sex
> - asking in-laws to stop giving advice
> - firing an employee
> - revealing a damaging secret that you have kept from someone close to you
> - political discussion with someone who defends a different position

Sometimes communication is difficult because of fear or an unwillingness to face potential adverse consequences. I admit I have not always faced my issues head-on. When drinking, I often hoped that others would never find out about what I had done. Looking back, my relations with others would not have been so significantly harmed if I had admitted my wrongs sooner. This was certainly true before I started making amends to those I had harmed. Today my AA tenth step nips issues in the bud if I am willing to "continue to take personal inventory and when I am wrong promptly admit it." Several of my failed relationships happened because I lacked the tools to effectively address ongoing differences of opinion.

Alcoholics Anonymous literature does a very good job giving specific directions on how to get and stay sober. At least for the "amend" steps, 9 and 10, there is not a lot provided in the AA literature on specifics for what to say during difficult conversations. I rely on my sponsor for that advice, but what happens when I am during a critical conversation and do not know how to proceed? I came across three areas of focus that pose questions that I believe will guide me as I navigate the stormy seas of difficult conversations. Douglas Stone, in his book *Difficult Conversations,* identifies the following three different types of conversations:

> the "What happened?" conversation
> the feelings conversation
> the identity conversation

Answers to all three types of conversations may not be required for every difficult conversation, but insights that the answers provide may hasten better outcomes for most encounters.

The "What Happened?" Conversation. The "What happened?" answers speak to the facts of any event from the perspectives of the individuals involved. Opinions often vary, but those individual perspectives are often prejudiced by bias. There are folks who may not say it outright, but they do not want to be confused by the facts because they have already made up their mind. I can think of an example.

I can recall a White House briefing by former President Trump, who was giving a press briefing with the members of the COVID-19 task force. Snopes confirmed that "US President Donald Trump suggested during a White House briefing "injecting disinfectants could treat COVID-19." The president's enemies jumped all over that statement as dangerous and fatal for anyone who might take the president's statement as a recommendation. The news later reported a person who ingested fish tank cleaner because the person reading the label saw something like hydroxychloroquine in the ingredients. Their fears were confirmed. People will die if they listen to the president. He must be stopped. He doesn't listen to the scientists. He is killing Americans.

Trump later walked the statement back, saying he was being sarcastic. He added, "It wouldn't be through injections but a cleaning and sterilization of an area. Maybe it works, maybe it doesn't work, but it would certainly have a big effect if it's a stationary object."

Some people say he was not advocating ingesting or injecting disinfectant but that science could investigate alternative cures with heat, light, etc. The intended message might have had more to do with brainstorming or thinking outside the box for solutions. Clearly the doctors on the team who were present must have taken it that way or they could have communicated the need for a retraction. The illustration points out that what is said and what is intended may be quite different.

Good communication skills are necessary for getting to the truth of what happened. If the facts matter, then we should say something like "Let's find sources we both respect and see if we can shed some more light on the subject." Or if there is continued difference of opinions, a person could say, "Hmmm. I guess I didn't interpret it that way. Here's how I recall it …"

I heard a wise person say that she thinks that there is a difference between "facts" and "truth." She said facts are things that exist, things that are known, like 2 plus 2 equals 4. She went on to say that truth can be a bit more flexible and that we each have and are seeking *our* truth. Our truth is not finite, but we have the ability not only to seek it but also change it as we grow intellectually and emotionally. Perhaps this distinction between "facts" and "truth" might be useful when discerning the "What happened?" conversation. It might be helpful when a person is at an impasse to say something like "I can tell that this is your truth, and I will not argue with how you might have arrived at that conclusion. My assessment is different from yours."

Bottom line, the dialogue must remain objective, free from rancor or prejudice. If the parties are either unable or unwilling to agree, then a person might say something like "It's clear we're at an impasse; can we agree to disagree? I value our relationship more than the need to be right."

The Feelings Conversations. Emotions happen. Visits to my psychiatrist confirmed that I needed to get in touch with my feelings. It seemed like everything I shared in group therapy was followed by the doctor's question "How does that make you feel?"

I admit that my untreated alcoholism squashed the ability to feel much of anything except anger and fear. One of the first indications that the fog of alcohol was starting to lift after I stopped drinking was that

I was able to feel again. At first, I cried at the drop of a hat. I suspected that my tear ducts were suddenly attached to my bladder. I bawled like a baby as a newcomer to AA, and since those first weeks in sobriety, I have observed that this first step of emoting is common in early recovery. They were tears of relief. I was filled with gratitude that I could begin to have authentic feelings.

I am a Detroit Lions fan, and those of us who even admit to loving them are likely to experience only two emotions: disgust and disappointment. If you are a Lions fan, it also helps if you have a sense of humor. The Lions notwithstanding, if I cannot identify with the lighter side of living, then life becomes a vale of tears. Being chronically depressed, it is easy for me to fall into depression, which in its deepest form can cause isolation and despair. But there are so many more emotions and gradations of each. What I have learned is that getting along with others and still having emotional integrity requires me to identify and own my emotions. And there are a lot of emotions to identify and own.

I have learned that emotions can be quite varied. There are emotions like adoration, aesthetic appreciation, empathetic pain, entrancement, nostalgia, romance, sexual desire, sympathy, and triumph.

I have to say it's been a while since I have felt entrancement. Perhaps if I follow the law of attraction I could send "entrancement" vibes into the universe and receive them back in kind. Entrancing notion!

Strangely there was one word I saw missing from the list and I wondered why. The word is *love*. Apparently, love isn't an emotion. I guess Tina Turner was right in when she sang, "It's just a secondhand emotion."

How do feelings fit into my desire to communicate more effectively? And what are the differences between feelings and emotions?

When people use the words *feeling* and *emotion,* are they interchangeable? I have heard that feelings like joy, sadness, happiness, anger, surprise, anxiety, etc. are responses to my senses, what I hear, taste, smell, touch, and feel. The numerous emotions I experience are more deep-seated and may exist to one degree or another in my mind because of my reactions over time. Would it be more effective for my psychiatrist to ask, "How does that make you emote?" rather than "How does that make you feel?" It makes sense to me to get to the core of my more deep-seated emotions if I am to be free from those that keep me from serenity.

The real issue regarding effective communication is this: how do I respond to my feelings during my interactions with others? It depends. I am coming to believe that I will let my feelings emerge so that I can own them without blocking transition to my rational thoughts. If the conversation is a difficult one, I must be true to myself and my feelings without sacrificing my ability to dialogue thoughtfully.

When dealing with feelings during difficult conversations, it is essential to clarify what I see and hear. I accept that I cannot tell anyone else how they should feel. Their feelings are their own. However, I shouldn't ignore or discount their feelings either, particularly if this aids authentic dialogue. If appropriate, I might acknowledge suspected feelings like sadness or anger. I might say something like "I can see that you're upset" or "It seems like I might have hit a nerve. Have I said something that offended you? I would only share my observation if it would aid my intent to offer empathy and sensitivity and to avoid escalation to conflict."

Regarding my own feelings, I must be just as straightforward. I need to clarify what someone has said to avoid any misinterpretation or misunderstanding. I do not want to overreact. I might say something like "I am confused when you say that I don't ever listen to you. Would you give me a specific example of when I didn't listen?"

For some difficult conversations, I will not be able to resolve all differences. I believe that progress counts and sometimes I will have to be satisfied with being able to clear the air a little.

I need to remember that during these difficult dialogues, I must avoid rancor at all costs. Rather than fuel an escalation during disagreements, I may say something like "You may be right. I guess time will tell" or "Can we agree to disagree? We clearly see things differently, but can we leave the discussion with the things we see in common?" If a conversation becomes too heated, I am no longer in solution, but I am likely adding to the problem. I may have to defer the discussion with something like "This is getting serious. I think we should hit the pause button on this conversation until we have had a chance to cool down. I value your friendship more than the need to be right."

Finally, I do not have to continue dialogue with anyone who becomes abusive or belligerent. If the other party is no longer willing or able to address differences with civility and at least the same amount of desire for resolution as I am, then I give myself permission to walk away. I am also learning to set boundaries with people to protect healthy relationships.

I have a sponsee who has befriended another individual I know in the program. My sponsee shared that his friend has been verbally abusive and overbearing during recent interactions. The criticism and anger were inappropriate and my sponsee finally said that if his friend wouldn't modify his behavior, he would not associate with him further. They have since gone their separate ways.

The Identity Conversation. This is perhaps the most difficult element to address during critical or difficult conversations. I hear friends talking about traumatic times in their childhood when their parents would tell them that they would never amount to anything good. It may not have been said directly, but the memory of what happened, real or imagined, has had a lasting impact.

Similar events shaped my feelings of self-worth and identity. When faced with challenging dialogue today, do I let these self-doubts affect my ability to interact? It is imperative for me to get an accurate assessment of my strengths and weakness. My AA program has steps for just this purpose. I have taken an inventory of my grosser handicaps and have asked God to remove my shortcomings. I no longer must be bogged down with selfishness, dishonesty, resentment, and fear. I have made direct amends to people I have harmed, and I continue to own my behavior daily. I no longer focus solely on my character defects, but I have identified, and I am growing my reliance on, my character assets. I continue to pray daily for knowledge of God's will for me and the power to carry that out. Doing this is changing me. I am neither cocky nor afraid. This practice gives me a quiet confidence to accept and react maturely when attacked. When challenged with attacks on my credibility or character, I can discern whether the problem is real or imagined, and if real, I am getting better at identifying whether the problem is mine or belongs to the other person(s). I am achieving a certain level of humility and in receipt of the gift of serenity to accept the things I cannot change and the courage to change the things I can. Finally, if there is one word that sums up the state of my identity it would be *humility*. If I let God direct my will and my life, all my conversations will be less difficult.

The important thing for me to remember is that I may not like the process or even be that successful with any outcomes intended. Fear may block my intention to engage or my progress in following through. Like my program, the acronym FEAR might take two different directions: face everything and recover or forget everything and run. I recently heard another meaning for the acronym that I really like: I forgot everything is all right. This is so true. After all, if I have turned my life and will over to the care of my God, everything will be all right. It is so important for me to overcome fear. My Alcoholics Anonymous *Twelve Steps and Twelve Traditions* book states, "Self-centered fear is the chief activator of all my defects of character." If I permit fear to grow unchecked, it can lead to anger and resentment. I recently heard the following humorous illustration in an AA meeting that makes this point.

> Fear: I'm worried I won't get my way.
> Anger: I discover I am not going to get my way.
> Resentment: I remember I did not get my way.

The skills I use to stay with the dialogue are worth the effort to learn and to practice. Sometimes just sustaining the dialogue is enough. Like the Nike ad suggests, "Just do it!"

I have a recent example of a difficult conversation that had to do with membership at our church. Due to the COVID-19 pandemic, my governor called for mandates that restricted some forms of public gatherings and others to be canceled entirely. Our church adapted this decree by offering virtual church via video and canceled public gatherings for a period. Our governor extended the mandates several times. Each extension was followed by outcries by members of churches who think that church attendance, with all the social distancing requirements, should be considered essential business, just as much as liquor stores, abortion clinics, and marijuana dispensaries. I saw numerous pastors on the news nationwide who were suggesting civil disobedience to protest what they thought was a violation of our constitutional rights. After my wife and I heard this news along with our governor's newest extension of the lock down, I wondered if our church would be part of the outcry to reconvene worship. I mentioned that I doubted it and added that I no longer felt part of the congregation. I told her that I felt excluded based on my political preferences. We talked about other churches of our denomination that might be a little more welcoming and none of the churches met the criteria my wife required. The discussion dissolved into my outcry that I would just quit going to church. Rather than remaining engaged with what was a difficult conversation, I quickly backpedaled and said that we should just forget talking about it. My wife responded, "That's what you always do when we face difficult decisions." Ouch. That hit me right between the eyes. Back to the drawing board. We will continue to dialogue, and I will practice good communication technique without forgetting everything and running.

We have since left that church, but we are exploring other options. I am grateful to have a wife who holds me accountable for staying engaged during difficult conversations.

I am also grateful for the confidence I am gaining because of my pursuit of emotional sobriety. I am coming to believe that I really am a competent, good person who is worthy of love. I am gaining the confidence to believe that future difficult conversations will not so negatively impact my self-image, self-esteem, or future well-being. During future difficult conversations, I will be more balanced and not so off-center and anxious. I will try not to take things so seriously.

6

Changing My Mind

Neuroplasticity

Neuroplasticity is the ability of the brain to change over time. I often wonder how much better my faculties would be if I had not destroyed so many brain cells because of drinking. I am grateful that the brain can regenerate cells. Thank You, God, for that restorative gift. Physically, God was doing for me what I could not do for myself. I suspect that if I had continued to drink longer, I may have damaged my brain permanently. I recently had a sponsee die from the complications of stage 4 wet brain. It affected his ability to think clearly, his speech, and his ability to walk and move. He died from complications of this malady. He literally forfeited his neuroplasticity because of his drinking and drugging.

It was thought that the brain stopped growing sometime in childhood, but that is no longer true. The brain has an amazing ability to regenerate even after head trauma. The brain replaces the capability lost in a damaged portion of the brain to be moved to another healthy segment of the brain. God is good, and He did an amazing job creating us the way He did.

Scientists have discovered that our bodies can promote the growth of brain-derived neurotropic factor (BDNF). BDNF promotes the growth of new synaptic connections and bolsters the strength of neuron signal transmission. However, stress and severe depression have now been determined to deplete neuroplasticity. Aerobic exercise for one hour for five of seven days has been shown to beneficial in growing BDNF. So running or biking is just as good for the brain as it is for the heart. There are other actions that are good for the brain, including the following:

- meditation
- educational pursuits
- playing, having fun
- replacing negativity with positivity
- being around positive thinking people

My psychiatrist prescribes drugs for my depression that chemically improve neuroplasticity. My depression kept me trapped in negativity and fear. I was limiting my brain's ability to recover from adversity and setbacks. I believe that one of the best ways to "change my mind" started with my work in psychotherapy.

Psychotherapy started centuries ago with origin credit going to philosophers called Stoics. I have a hard time envisioning a philosopher reclining on a couch while talking about their deepest darkest secrets. One of them might have had a scroll to take notes and add follow-up questions like "So how did that make you feel?" Those Stoics are given partial credit as the originators of what is now called cognitive behavioral therapy (CBT). Socrates and Epicurus believed that their philosophic efforts were in fact therapeutic. It appears they were correct. These guys were the forbearers of a rational approach to psychic and emotional problems.

Stoicism originated way back in the third century AD. That philosophical approach sounds strangely like what Buddhists practice. Like Buddhists, they felt that we should not allow any of the outside influences of pleasure or even pain to distract us needlessly. They preached living in the now and accepting life on life's terms. Hmmmm. This also sounds a lot like what is stressed in my AA program. The Stoics lived virtuous lives and were good students of nature. Just think: I could have been a Stoic, and at some level I believe I am.

The credit for Stoicism's origin has been given to a philosopher by the name of Zeno of Citium. Zeno said that to live well, we must exhibit mental strength to not be seduced by the things of the world and not fall victim to the outward pleasures of the world, nor should we fear death. We should live in the moment and accept that life is impermanent. And through the acquisition of knowledge, we have an ability to develop ethical character. Could this be philosophical plagiarism? I wonder because it sounds very similar to Buddhist philosophy. Stoicism thrived until Christianity started flourishing in the fourth century. This passage in the New Testament parallels Stoicism's suggestion to not fall for the desires of the flesh:

> Do not love the world or anything in the world. If anyone loves the world, love for the Father is not in them.
> For everything in the world—the lust of the flesh, the lust of the eyes, and the pride of life—comes not from the Father but from the world.
> The world and its desires pass away, but whoever does the will of God lives forever. (1 John 2:15–17 NIV)

Another more modern example of Stoicism can be traced back to a guy by the name of Reinhold Niebuhr. As an alcoholic, I am quite familiar with the prayer he wrote back in 1934.

> God give me the serenity to accept the things I cannot change; the courage to change the things I can; and the wisdom to know the difference.

I want to emphasize that I am not a psychiatrist, nor am I offering any psychiatric advice. What I am exploring and offering in this book are some of the tools I have personally used or experienced and found helpful, along with some that I am not familiar with but intend to explore with an open mind.

Cognitive Behavioral Therapy

My first association with psychiatry was as a patient in group therapy. My psychiatrist must have been trained in Freudian psychiatric method because he focused on uncovering unconscious events of my past and how surfacing a forgotten early life trauma may have caused my inability to cope. I didn't give this first experience an honest effort because I was drinking heavily and did not disclose this to the psychiatrist or my group during my treatment. I spent a lot of time and the insurance company's money to reveal a couple events of my upbringing that yielded some insight regarding events of my past that might have caused trauma. However, that awareness was not sufficient to deal with my real problem: alcohol. Alcoholics Anonymous led me to finally getting honest about my problem.

Cognitive behavioral therapy seems like a pragmatic and practical way to assist with being more able to face life on life's terms. This form of psychotherapy works on changing thought patterns to change moods and behaviors. Rather than problems being attributed to unconscious forces from the past, it focuses on current distorted beliefs or thoughts that affect negative thoughts and actions.

The primary reason I am attracted to CBT as one of the tools for improving emotional sobriety is that it works.

CBT focuses less on uncovering unconscious traumatic events of my past and more on recent thought and behavioral patterns that need to be addressed to achieve a better life. And while one might benefit from working with a psychiatrist or therapist, there are several CBT tools that do not require any outside help. In fact, unbeknownst to me, I have been practicing several of the recommended CBT actions with my habits I learned in Alcoholics Anonymous (AA).

AA and CBT

Here are some of the ways that my AA teachings match CBT suggestions. CBT can be useful for identifying and changing behavior that may no longer be contributing to a healthy emotional life. While I have not perfected these techniques, I can endorse them based on how they have contributed to my personal growth.

Journaling. I have had numerous periods in my sober life where I found it helpful to write a daily journal. Just like all other inventory work, it helps to get the events of the day down in black and white. It serves three purposes. First, I can see any patterns of behavior that may be detrimental. Second, it helps me identify and own up to my part of any troubles I may be having with others. I am then able to see the cause and effect of how my feelings and behaviors are related. Finally, I can start to see the progress of any solutions that I am attempting to practice in all my affairs.

Relaxation and stress reduction. If I am in a prolonged period of stress, I can spend some quiet time in prayer and meditation. I can repeat the Serenity Prayer until I am feeling relief. "God, grant me the serenity to accept the things I cannot change, the courage to change the things I can, and the wisdom to know the difference." This prayer is also useful to discern whether a problem is mine or someone else's.

I can practice deep breathing exercises to slow my thoughts and heart rate. I can take a deep breath and hold it for a slow count to ten. I slowly exhale for another count to ten. I then repeat the process. I have discovered this aids relaxation as well as helping me to get to sleep quicker. Others have found that this breathing exercise can lower blood pressure.

Move a muscle, change a thought. Exercise is therapeutic. A short walk or a bike ride can change an outlook. If I catch myself thinking negatively, I can choose to think about something else. Like my friend in AA advised, "Move a muscle; change a thought." A combination of walking and meditation, also called "mindful walking," can unite the body and the mind. It can also produce endorphins that can reduce pain and produce a feeling of euphoria.

Affirmations. I can repeat positive statements when I am feeling self-defeated or depressed, such as the following:

> ➤ "I am a child of God."
> ➤ "God has chosen me to be his own."
> ➤ "I am much loved and cared for."
> ➤ "I am doing God's will."
> ➤ "I have nothing to fear."
> ➤ "God is my fortress and my strength."

I heard a pastor recently talk about the power of words, particularly spoken words. He suggested that there was a correlation between positive words and positive outcomes. Conversely, there is a correlation between negative words and negative or even harmful outcomes. If I have negative thoughts, it is better to keep those thoughts to myself. My mother used to say, "If you don't have anything good to say, don't say anything at all." The pastor went on to say that if I share my negative thoughts out loud, I risk what could become a self-fulfilling prophecy. Statements like "I'm never going to get that job" or "I'm never going to lose weight" unwittingly become my intentions. When I voice these negative thoughts out loud, my words become my prophecy. Is it possible that I get the unintended consequences I am trying to avoid?

Self-compassion. There are times when I need to cut myself some slack. Like an AA told me years ago, "Quit beating yourself up." I can assess whether I have done the best I can and learn to accept the outcome even if it does not meet my perfectionistic expectations. I can lighten up on my self-critique. I am learning that if I can't forgive myself, I will never be able to forgive others.

Addressing negative thought patterns. I can evaluate my tendencies to drift back into gloom-and-doom thinking by forecasting disasters that may never materialize. I must remember one of the acronyms for fear: FEAR. (false evidence appearing real). Thoughts of morbidity and awfulizing lead to paralyzing fear and isolation. I must remember though that I can only address those things that I am *willing to own and admit*. If I am unable to rigorously review my thought patterns and work to adjust my attitude, I had better be willing to seek outside help from a therapist.

Pause when agitated. I need to take time to move from an emotional response to a rational one. This is easy for me to say but hard to do. Taking a few minutes to assess a situation permits me to determine what is real and what is false. I can then respond rationally as opposed to emotionally. A technique I use, when I have the presence of mind to do so, is to ignore my first thought. Taking time to think before I act saves me a lot of grief and preempts actions that may harm others or myself, particularly in tense situations. When I pause, I am better able to go through my mental list of criteria: Is my response true? Is it kind? Is it necessary?

Move the focus from self. Turn my thoughts and energies toward helping someone else. Working with another alcoholic can help when all other methods fail.

Qualified CBT Therapists

There are other practical CBT activities that may require help from a qualified therapist. Under a psychiatrist's care, I have experienced the first three of four techniques listed here.

Cognitive restructuring. A therapist can assist in identifying tendencies to jump to false conclusions or assuming the worst. The therapist can assist in identifying negative thoughts or patterns that become self-fulfilling.

Role-Playing. This is helpful in identifying new ways to practice key conversations and improve confidence in addressing various situations that have been troublesome in the past.

Guided Discovery. Through observation and questioning, a therapist can challenge one's thinking and offer alternatives to the beliefs that may not be true or, at a minimum, beliefs that no longer serve their purpose. I found this technique effective while working as a facilitator and consultant.

Exposure Therapy. The therapist may be able to help identify the patterns of behavior that provoke fear and anxiety and help with one's confidence and ability to cope.

Neurolinguistic Programming (NLP)

Another contemporary therapy for my transformation to emotional maturity is neurolinguistic programing (NLP). Like the tools suggested so far, it is behavioral in nature and focuses on changing behavior that no longer works.

Neurolinguistic programing (NLP) stresses the use of language to respond to neurological stimuli. NLP challenges the way a person responds to stimulus to identify behavior that better achieves that person's goals. It helps to develop better choices with the words they use and the body language they display. If a person's thought process leads them to erroneous decisions, then NLP can retrain the brain to choose better and to ultimately to behave better. NLP is about retraining and learning ways to better communicate.

Are there similarities to AA? Like AA, NLP guides the practitioner to change their attitudes about the world and the people in it rather than trying to change the world. I may not be able to change what happens in the world, but I can change how I react to what happens in the world.

I will keep an open mind to avoid contempt prior to investigation. Is it possible for NLP to literally "change one's mind"? If it can provide another way for me to give up my old ideas and focus on better ways to think and act, then it may be worth consideration.

Many of us in AA have heard that the only thing we can really change is ourselves and our attitudes. Many times though, it is easier to identify the need for an attitude adjustment in others than in ourselves.

I heard a young lady share during an Alcoholics Anonymous *Twelve Steps and Twelve Traditions* meeting. She shared that she was having a very difficult time emotionally. She didn't go into the details initially except to say that she was having a very hard time coping with challenges she faced because of COVID-19.

She had called her mom earlier in the day and told her that she wanted to put her stuff in storage and move in with her for a while. Her mom responded with a definite no and stated that she would not be sharing her home with anyone. My AA friend proceeded to recount how she thought her mom was playing favorites with her sister.

Apparently, the sister has a gambling addiction and had recently cashed in an IRA to pay off a large gambling debt. Mom insisted that she would not enable the sister with any financial aid, but she ended up cosigning a loan for a top-of-the-line Jeep.

You could see from my AA friend's face that she was not taking the perceived injustice well. After some more complaining about her problems, she paused. She remained quiet for a while and then requested if she could reread the Prayer of St. Francis from the *Twelve Steps and Twelve Traditions* out loud.

After she finished, her whole demeanor changed. Her facial expression softened. She said that while she hadn't had any religious training in her upbringing, she was beginning to get the idea that she may need some spiritual help. Amazing! In the span of a few minutes, she had a change in attitude. She literally changed her mind. AA made this possible.

There is a lot to unpack learning the vocabulary and activities involved with practicing NLP. I am reading *Neuro-Linguistic Programing for Dummies*. It does provide an overview in layman's terms of what NLP is and how it works.

I do have some reservations. One online NLP source offered training and trainer/specialist certification for 40 percent off the regular price. Another online source offered training on conversational hypnosis. What is conversational hypnosis? A critic implied that even though NLP has no scientific basis or validation, it might be useful for learning communication techniques to improve sales and productivity. Does this mean that you can use NLP to get people to do what you want them to do? Critics say it takes six years or more to become a psychologist, but you can become a certified NLP expert in five weeks. Other critics say there is no evidence, other than anecdotal, to suggest it works.

Other Less Conventional Solutions

There are other techniques being used in addition to those I have mentioned, and based on the numbers of people who are attracted to them, there is quite a demand. Psychiatry is a relatively new science, and thankfully there are evolving modern solutions that show great promise. Not all the techniques have much science behind them, and sadly people with significant need will be attracted to solutions without proven efficacy.

One such method I discovered is called the Silva Mind Control Method. A book with the same title has been written by Jose Silva and Philip Miele. The book describes various outcomes of those who practice the method, including improving one's eyesight, losing weight, better memory, and numerous other miraculous accomplishments. It is a combination of meditation and something akin to self-hypnosis. There are courses taught by "expert" practitioners who claim to shorten the time it takes to be proficient. Students are taught how to get from a "beta mind state," the one we have when we are awake, to an "alpha brain state" that helps use more of the brain's full capacity. This alpha brain state along with various states of visualization helps practitioners to be more focused and productive, by tapping into a "higher intelligence." Addicts can fall prey to easy solutions. Many seek the easier softer way.

Can science offer any solutions for changing minds? Who wouldn't like the immediate gratification that might be available from inserting miniscule, programmed robots? Some futurists predict the creation of "nano bots" that could be injected to monitor and automatically alter moods. Currently there are drugs to control moods and mitigate negative behavior. However, many are highly addictive and come with numerous side effects. What about better living through chemistry or maybe even reengineering? Perhaps there will be drugs or even surgery that will eliminate all forms of mental diseases.

Remember the movie *Stepford Wives,* which replaced wives with robots who were more submissive to their husbands? I wonder how long in today's "cancel culture" for this movie to be "canceled." Perhaps science will one day create a medication that will be harmless but still effective, and it may be closer than ever to achieve that goal. What about the possibility of getting to the source and altering DNA to create a more perfect human? This isn't some futuristic science fiction creation. It's happening now. There is also talk of something called a "god" hat that could be worn to stave off negative emotions by electronically altering brain waves. Maybe that's not so far-fetched. Recently there have been encouraging results from tests that involved stimulating the brains of heroin-addicted rats with electrodes.

With all its intendent misery and suffering, I hope that humankind will accept their reality and take steps to work with what they were given. I am determined to gain my relational sobriety by using the traditional and proven methods suggested in this book. I do not want to be some drugged-up cyborg facsimile. I want to become the best version of me—the one that God intended. That is the one I want to bring to all my relationships. Al-Anon is one such known solution that I may have "half measured" in the past. It worked, but I faltered before I had an Al-Anon spiritual awakening.

Al-Anon

I came to AA through the Al-Anon program. My wife was being treated for alcoholism at an in-house treatment facility and I discovered that the whole family would be involved in the treatment program. I found out during the family orientation program that I was a *prime enabler* and *codependent*. While I could stay at home for the one-month program, I was told that all family members could not drink for the time my wife was in treatment and that I should start attending meetings of Al-Anon. I found out that Al-Anon is a mutual support organization for the families and friends of alcoholics, especially those of members of Alcoholics Anonymous. OK, I was willing to do that if it helped my wife. As it turned out, it was only for a month, at least initially.

I followed the recommendation and did attend Al-Anon meetings. I did not fit in well there. Here were spouses of alcoholics who seemed decimated over their significant others' drinking. They cried, wailed, and shared comforting slogans like "Release them with love," "Keep an open mind," and "Feel good about saying no." They had the three C's: "You didn't cause it, you can't control it, and you can't cure it." They said, "Angels exist, but since some of them don't have wings, we call them friends." I would see them cry and console each other and would think, *Lighten up a bit. How bad can this really be?*

I had contempt prior to investigation. But as they say in AA, more will be revealed. I had additional experiences with Al-Anon in California. There was men's group that met regularly and since I already knew many of the men who also attended Alcoholics Anonymous, I felt comfortable sharing and learning from about all aspects of their recovery, particularly in their sober relationships. I really liked the camaraderie, and attending the meetings helped me to relate better with my wife and family. Even though the sharing was at times intense, there was much levity. I never will forget an AA/Al-Anon friend who used to say prior to holidays, "Yeah, this holiday would be great if it weren't for the "crazy loved ones." Everyone howled with laughter, but you could tell he wasn't serious as he was one of the pillars of spirituality for that meeting.

Later there were married couples who were sober and, like my wife and me, even had the same sobriety dates. We attended monthly couples AA/Al-Anon meetings and the sharing there was inciteful and helpful. But how does one know whether one is codependent? Here are some descriptors that confirmed my qualification:

> people pleaser
> happiness is dependent on another person
> confuses love with pity
> fear of abandonment
> intimacy issues
> constant review of mistakes, thinking that something could have been done to avoid them
> difficulty in communicating thoughts honestly
> difficulty in saying no to requests
> emotionally overreactive
> need to take care of those around me
> feeling responsible for the actions of others
> inability to detach

I can say that several of these codependent descriptors apply to me, even after over three decades of sobriety. My thinking still requires daily adjustment, particularly in my old ideas about marriage. My wife has the same sobriety date, and I can attest to the fact that she is working daily to keep her thinking on track. We both pray for our Higher Power to guide our thinking.

Codependent marriages like mine require individual growth if we are to bring our best selves to our relationship.

As an alcoholic and narcissist, I know there is room for improvement. I demand much from others and sometimes feel I am entitled to more than I deserve. I can be charming and often make a good first impression. I sometimes pretend to care about the feelings of others, but when put to the test, I am only able to sustain the charade for as long as they were willing to give me what I wanted.

I'm not using this as an excuse, but I see others in AA that exhibit these behaviors. That does not mean that all alcoholics are narcissistic, nor does it mean that all narcissists are alcoholic. It is a real challenge, however, for a narcissist to live and let live or become emotionally sober.

Sadly, my list of afflictions is growing. Based on my current assessment, I am a recovering chronically depressed, neurotic, narcissistic, codependent, workaholic, shopaholic, drug addict, and sex addict alcoholic. Fortunately, I am doing the work needed to recover. I may still have these afflictions, but most of the manifestations are in remission, thanks to God, Alcoholics Anonymous, and help from a psychiatrist. My morning prayer includes my request to become more like my Lord and Savior, Jesus Christ. I can attest to the miracles of divine intervention. God is doing for me what I cannot do for myself.

Personal Experiences with Therapy

Many years ago, I succumbed to my wife's request/ultimatum to see a psychiatrist. She had been seeing her psychiatrist for a while and suggested that if our marriage was going to remain intact, I had better look at my part in our disunion.

I was still drinking heavily at the time but selfishly decided that seeing a psychiatrist would be cheaper than giving her 50 percent of everything I owned. Always thinking of the easier, softer way, I decided to just go to my wife's psychiatrist. After meeting him, I decided that this wouldn't be that bad after all. He was an imposing figure with a wild mane of hair and dressed more like a hippie than a doctor. He rode a motorcycle and would park it inside the building near the stairs that went up to the lobby of the building where he had his offices. The group sessions were conducted in a very chic and modern room that was luxuriously appointed with expensive leather furniture. It was on a high floor in a high rise with overly high ceilings and expansive glass windows. This all permitted a premium view of the surrounding city, and first impressions were this was going to be expensive. My second impression was that this would be a comfortable place to whine for an hour or two each week. Fortunately my insurance covered the fees.

I wasn't sure what to expect, but I discovered that the good doctor was able to drag the parts of my past out of me that I needed to face considering the current reality. Yes, there was much discussion of the patterns of behavior that seemed most harmful along with how past relationships may have contributed to current behavior choices. And while the sessions enabled much discovery as to the origin of my neurosis, they were only able to go as far as my level of honesty would permit. As a practicing alcoholic, I was unable to muster enough of the truth necessary to solve any of my relationship problems. I never shared how much I drank. So that little fact and how it may have contributed to my problems was never addressed.

I must have fooled my group therapy mates enough to suggest that I was ready for "termination." The good doctor agreed with their assessment, and we scheduled a termination party. Oh, and alcohol was not only permitted, but it was also expected. What did I do? Well, what does one drink during such an auspicious occasion? Champagne. I brought enough champagne for everyone to get as high as they cared to. Funny thing though. The other groupies weren't the slightest bit interested in getting drunk. I poured the bubbly and lifted my glass to toast the contributors to celebrate my return to normalcy, and in the process, I preceded to spill my drink. As I was toasting, my hand was shaking so much that I was spilling the contents. I was not insightful enough at the time to know the reason for the tremors. I know now that it was due to my dishonesty. I had not been honest enough to admit that my real problem was right there in my hand for everyone to see. Alcohol. Alcohol was my master, and I was unwilling at the time to admit it.

Was it entirely unsuccessful? No. Although, despite my failure to disclose a key piece of the puzzle, I did have some breakthroughs. I did achieve some help from psychotherapy.

- I got to know myself a little better.
- I became aware of childhood trauma that may have contributed to lifelong misconceptions.
- I discovered misperceptions regarding my parents' role in my disease.
- I identified factors in my past that limited my ability to cope.
- I discovered that I wasn't alone; others had the same issues.

> ➤ I confirmed that there were solutions to enable me to better cope with my neurosis.

> ➤ I did alleviate some of my emotional pain.

Because I was not honest about revealing my drinking habits, I held onto one of the characteristics that many alcoholics share. I was a victim, or more accurately, I used victimhood as a major cause of my discomfort. I would whine that it was my father's fault. He was too strict. He was not emotionally available for me. He demanded too much and was hypercritical. By today's standards, I could claim he was physically abusive. He spanked me and laid his hands on me when I disobeyed. Of course, most of my assessment was overblown, but it did provide a convenient scapegoat for why I behaved the way I did and why I felt I was able to justify my heavy drinking.

I held these resentments well into my first couple of years of sobriety. And while I eventually did a fourth step inventory and made direct amends to my father, it wasn't until I had another trip to a psychologist with my wife that I had a significant and life-view changing breakthrough.

It started when my wife and I were going through another rough patch in our relationship and we were directed by a friend to a psychologist. He was a practitioner of imago therapy. The psychologist told me that imago therapy could help couples in committed relationships to work out their issues and to find better ways to communicate to find common ground. It could help me to identify how childhood experiences influence how I behave and how I respond to others in adult relationships.

After a couple of sessions together, the psychologist asked to meet with me alone. Apparently, the problem wasn't with my wife after all. I was sure that it was either her inability or unwillingness to do her part in our marriage. She just couldn't understand what I needed from her! I was told later that mind reading was not part of her skill set.

I complied with the doctor's request but was sure that he had missed the cues I had communicated regarding my wife's obvious faults. He had not missed anything. In fact, he didn't want to talk about my wife at all. He asked me to talk about my childhood. Of course, I was eager to tell him what a mean man my father had been. He listened and asked me to go deeper into my feelings. Unbeknownst to me, I had considerable anger.

The doctor was patient but methodical. I remember a lot of tears and pillow punching. It finally came down to my description of a twisted vine with numerous sharp thorns. I told him that I felt like I was in shackles and that I was trying to break free. This was followed with more pillow punching and a torrent of tears.

As the sessions progressed, I talked less about my father and more about myself. It took a while, but I eventually discovered that my father had been doing the best he knew how to do. Eventually, I came to see my father the way he truly was. The anger subsided and the relief was profound. That part of me that had grown misshapen from my distortions started to come into correct focus. The mistaken recollections were replaced by a more honest awareness.

I was growing up. I finally was able to enjoy a more mature attitude toward a father that I grew to love more each day for the rest of his life. I was able to make direct amends to him, this time focusing on my regrets for not upholding my part of a father/son relationship.

To the end of his life, I was able to repair the relationship that I had damaged. In addition to the restoration of the relationship with my father, I was finally able to see my part in my marital issues. It was easier now to own my shortcomings, and my wife and I became closer once again. None of this would have been possible without the successful psychotherapy.

I have come to believe that there are three focus areas that must be employed to reach my goal of live and let live: rational, emotional, and spiritual. However, success in just two of three focus areas will not be sufficient to achieve emotional sobriety.

My journey has so far explored the rational and emotional focus areas. While I have learned much from covering those two areas, I know that it will be work on the spiritual focus area that may have the most potential for personal growth.

7

Spiritually Awake

I often hear people talk about their various paths to a "spiritual awakening." Though the paths differ, those completing the Twelve Steps of Alcoholics Anonymous arrive at a spiritual destination of their own understanding. Even those who question religion or even the existence of God are trying to seek something beyond themselves. These individuals often report that it was in AA they found their Higher Power. Many have rejected the religion of their upbringing, but all who sincerely seek a Higher Power usually find some source that enables them to achieve a new state of consciousness and being.

Alcoholics are free to choose their own conception of a Higher Power. Their choices are as varied as the members themselves. It seems that everyone in our clan is in search of a power beyond themselves. They may not be comfortable with a religious definition of God, but they invariably find something they can rely on: GOD, meaning group of drunks or good orderly direction. I heard a new acronym during a recent meeting: guidance over defiance. The meeting attendees who were there immediately started nodding their heads up and down in agreement. Alcoholics must give up fighting and accept help to permit the *guidance* to begin. That decision to surrender becomes the beginning for our relief from *defiance* and moves us to *reliance*. This *reliance* leads us to not only change our minds but just as importantly permits us to open our hearts.

Seeking Enlightenment

Looking back at the '60s Woodstock photos, the event portrayed thousands of young people gathered for one common purpose: to enjoy music and drug-induced messages of peace and love. It was an interesting dichotomy. Lacking any significant preparation and presented with fields of mud deluged with rain, the revelers stayed true to their quest and were genuinely united as a massive tribute to mind over matter. Maybe it was the sex, drugs, and rock and roll that permitted them to prevail. Perhaps the crowds were determined to fulfill their expectations. Was there some form of group consciousness that made it so?

I believe they were seeking something beyond hedonism. They may not have known exactly what it was that drew them to that pasture, but they were searching nonetheless. From the accounts told by the people who attended, it was magical and wondrous. It was indeed a once-in-a-lifetime experience. Could there have been a spiritual element? It makes me wonder about the power of thought and how thought and outcome are related. Those who gathered at Woodstock must have thought beforehand that it was going to be special and therefore it was.

The whole discussion of how mind and action are related is a rich topic for exploration. Is it possible to think my way into emotional integrity? Since all actions are preceded by thoughts, does that mean that if I think better, I will behave better? That might fly in the face of what I have heard during AA meetings where the senior statesmen might say something like "You have to act your way into right thinking; you can't think your way into right action."

Other AA, primarily the younger ones, say something quite different. When the topic includes discussions about spirituality, many of them shy away from following any suggestion that even sniffs of religiosity and say they will just focus on doing the next right thing.

What comes first: the thought or the action? Is just being "good," by doing the next right thing, good enough? Is just doing the next right thing enough to obtain a spiritual awakening? Or does one have to pray and meditate sufficiently to have a conscious contact with God as a prerequisite?

Perhaps I am making this more difficult than it needs to be. Maybe I should just stop worrying about my spiritual state and do what one of my favorite Bible verses suggests. "Be still and know that I am God" (Psalm 46:10 NLT). Another translation of the passage interprets it as "Cease striving and know that I am God!" (Psalm 46:10 ASB). Does that suggest that I need to stop working so hard? I have heard others suggest that I should focus on *just being*. After all, I'm a *human being,* not a *human doing*. Perhaps I should just focus on the present and only on what is. Should I just focus on my breathing? I might hear something like this:

> Let your breath be the focus on what is happening right now at this moment. Lift your arms all the way up. Concentrate on your breath. Breathe in your nostrils and out your nostrils slowly. Stretch your arms. Reach higher and higher. Feel the sensation. Rise up. All the way up onto your toes. On your toes.

I have seen the photos of people in meditation sitting cross-legged with their forefingers touching their thumbs in palms up position while uttering a resonant "*Ahhhh oooo mmmmmmm.*" I used to wonder just what, if anything good, could come from sitting and humming.

As I watch my wife going through the various poses, it really does seem that this is a manifestation of how body, mind, and spirit can be conjoined. Clearly this is more than just a stretching routine. My wife refers to this daily routine as her "practice." She is just one of many who do something similar as a path to enlightenment or least a lightening of burdens that keeps them from serenity. Is it possible she uses this "practice" to change or train the mind into right thinking?

Sustain the body. Clear the mind. Elevate the spirit. This certainly sounds like I could be onto something that could possibly lead to emotional integrity. Can it be done? This unification of body, mind, and spirit was the goal of the man who eventually became the Buddha.

The three key words that summarize this practice are *virtue, mindfulness,* and *wisdom*. I have heard virtue described as self-control of what one thinks, says, and does for good. Mindfulness is focused attention—attention to what I see around me and attention to what I see in myself. Wisdom is applied common sense. It is acquired though living and often by learning the hard way. Through trial and error, I learn from successes but also through pain. Over time, I can identify what I may do that hurts myself or others, and alternatively, I am able to identify what to do to help myself or others.

My goal is to achieve "liberating insight." I desire to finally be free to live in the world without fear. I can then be my true self without apology or rancor. I can *live and let live*. I will finally be able to bring my true self into relationships and not be overwhelmed by outside pressure to conform. Maybe this is what is meant by the suggestion to "wear the world like a loose garment." I will then be able to apply what I learn to enable a better and more useful life while at the same time remaining comfortable as *my authentic self*. This seems very practical. If I do not embrace virtue, mindfulness, and wisdom, will I ever be able to "do the next right thing"? Will I ever be able to live and let live? How did the Buddha achieve virtue, mindfulness, and wisdom? He did it by training his mind.

How can anyone become the person they were intended to be? Ironically, it must come from deep from within us by stressing positive thought and diminishing negative thought.

There is very little specific direction offered in the Big Book of Alcoholics Anonymous on how to achieve this inner clarity. There are general admonitions to pray and meditate but nothing so intense as to achieve the kind of transformation of mind and body achieved by the sages and saints of every religious tradition. Is it possible to be peaceful, radiant, and loving and at the same time be in touch with moment-to-moment reality? This is my goal.

The mood-altering chemicals I took to achieve this state of mind never worked. Ironically, what I was looking for was always there. I was just looking in the wrong places. The altered state I created with chemicals was far from the state of mind I desired. My inner truth was obscured by the "scatomas" caused by drinking and drugging. My addiction just hid the defects of character that kept me mired in bondage. I am now seeking to identify those things that keep me from my personal freedom.

The world keeps turning and changing, and I had better accept it for what it is. I cannot change the world. I cannot change my past, but I can improve my present. I can set the ball rolling in terms of the person I desire to be. I can lay the groundwork for emotional growth, but there are challenges. Like others, I have been in a pandemic caused by a very infectious virus. Some suggest it emanated from Wuhan, China. Regardless of the source, numerous lives have been lost so far in the US.

My governor extended a "shelter in place" mandate because she said it wasn't safe to go back to a normal existence. Social distancing, washing hands, and wearing protective masks were offered as the "new normal." Churches, gyms, hair salons, and movie theaters were closed. Sporting events and schools were closed, and it was uncertain when they would open completely. Air travel to other countries was restricted. The economy was decimated and at one point fell to 20 percent unemployment.

The scientists told us that people in my age group should continue to "shelter in place" even if the restrictions for others are lifted. This was to be my "new normal" until a vaccine or cure for COVID-19 was developed and approved. Thankfully, my wife and I have received the two vaccinations and a booster. Is this the beginning of a return to normal? Well, even after receiving all recommended doses of the vaccine, Dr. Fauci recommended that I continue wear a mask and follow the guidelines previously mandated.

During this same time frame, a white cop was accused and subsequently convicted of murdering a handcuffed black man. There were many protests that evolved to looting and rioting in several cities. The trial is over, and the jury was charged with determining innocence or guilt. The national guard treated Minneapolis like a war zone. Maxine Waters, a California representative, told Minnesotans to take to the streets if the cop wasn't convicted. Even after the conviction, the protests continued. Additionally, during this time frame, there was a highly contested and volatile presidential election. The election was won by the challenger, but a whole new set of issues exists. The country remains divided between those who see the incumbent as the answer and those who hate him. The left embraced violent protests in the name of justice but held a different standard to those who protested at the nation's Capital. The media called the protests by the left, mostly peaceful. Those on the right were called racist insurrectionists. What does this little slice of history suggest? Life is constantly changing and accepting life on life's terms is not always easy. As a result, throughout the history of the world, there has been suffering. This is nature's way. Nature continuously evolves, and our reaction to these changes sometimes is painful, and sometimes we suffer.

Suffer

to undergo or feel pain or distress: The patient is still suffering.

to sustain injury, disadvantage, or loss: One's health suffers from overwork. The business suffers from lack of capital.

to undergo a penalty, as of death: The traitor was made to suffer on the gallows.

to endure pain, disability, death, etc., patiently or willingly.

verb (used with object)

to undergo, be subjected to, or endure (pain, distress, injury, loss, or anything unpleasant): to suffer the pangs of conscience.

to undergo or experience (any action, process, or condition):

to suffer change (Source Dictionary.com)

I have had misconceptions about Buddhism. I had heard that Buddhism is all about suffering and that there is nothing you can do about suffering. I thought that their message is that you just have to grin and bear it. I have since found that that description is at best a bit simplistic and at worst quite inaccurate.

I talked to a Buddhist friend, and she told me that suffering should be understood in a broader sense. She said there is more to the definition of suffering than endurance of pain. She says that it comes from the word *dukkha,* which also can mean discontent, no matter how small. Suffering can include stress, dissatisfaction, and even unhappiness with a humdrum life.

I have heard AA say, "Pain is mandatory, but suffering is optional." There will always be pain and suffering. The degree to which I succumb to suffering is commensurate to how well I respond and adapt to change. I must do this to survive.

How can I achieve my goal to compensate for suffering? I can start by being kinder to others and kinder to myself. The antidote to suffering is compassion. I have come to believe that compassion for self is not selfish nor is it a form of self-pity. I am not feeling sorry for myself by showing self-compassion. Just as I would show compassion for others when I care for them and want the best for them in a nurturing caring way, I can show compassion for myself to alleviate my suffering. I can show myself warmth and self-comfort just as I would for others who need attention and care when they are suffering. After all, how would I treat a sick person? To me, compassion is a variant of empathy. If I can feel empathy for others, why can't I feel compassion for myself? I have a disease. I am a sick person. If empathy is an antidote to suffering, will I embrace it?

I have witnessed my share of suffering: emotional, physical, and spiritual. Whether it is the alcoholic or family members who are affected by the disease, the pain at times can be overwhelming. The alcoholic promises to stay sober and may do so for a period, but then at exactly the wrong time, he comes home drunk yet again. The spouse is justifiably angry. The following scenario is repeated often.

> She yells at him, "How could you? You promised you wouldn't drink again! You said you were going to AA meetings, but you haven't even been doing that have you? I told you if you came home drunk again I would take the kids and move in with my parents. I want a divorce!" The alcoholic responds with something like "Divorce! Go ahead and get a divorce. You're the reason I drink. You constantly nag and treat me like a child. You have no idea how much pressure I feel. How would you react if you could not get a job and no one would even give you a chance to work? You would drink too if you had my old boss. If he hadn't blackballed me, I would be able to at least get interviews. But you don't care."
>
> The yelling starts and the alcoholic strikes out at his wife. The kids try to protect their mother, and the alcoholic pushes one of the children out of the way; the child falls and hits his head. One of the other children calls the police, and yet again the police arrive. The alcoholic ends up in the back of the police car, and after a night in jail, he checks himself into a treatment center for the third time. Later, a person from child services arrives at the home and interviews the wife and children. The officer recommends to her superiors

that the children be taken from the home as the mother is also addicted to drugs.

What can be done to overcome this kind of suffering? The Buddha said he taught only suffering and the transformation of suffering. My goal is to acknowledge my own suffering but develop a course of action that can transform it into serenity.

A friend told me a story about his relationship with his sponsor in early sobriety. He said that he went to his sponsor's house one morning and commenced to unload a litany of problems that he was having. For each problem, the sponsor patiently offered a suggestion based on one of the Twelve Steps of the program. My friend was not receptive to any of the suggestions and offered more and more rationalizations as to why he couldn't follow the sponsor's suggestions. He finally asked the sponsor, "What should I do?" The sponsor said, "Well, you aren't willing to follow any of the suggestions I'm offering, so suffer."

It seems to me this is the crux of most of the "suffering" dilemmas. If I am unwilling to seek and take direction and be accountable for actions that are in my own best interest, then I too will continue to suffer.

I suffer from major depression. I have been under a psychiatrist's care for years. There are days at a time where it is not an issue and I can enjoy life despite the challenges that we all face from time to time. There are other times though that I suffer. It reappears out of the blue, and at times, it feels like I am in a dark tunnel with the walls coming in from all sides. There does not seem to be any consolation when I am in the depressive grip. I have come to identify the beginning shortly after the onset and have learned to do my very best to not let the depression overcome me. I cannot stop the feeling, but I can own it and work through it. I can temper and possibly mitigate the darkest and deepest depths of my depression. I pray. I breathe. I focus on the reality around me. I tell myself that this is something that can be endured and that I am not alone. I have a wife who understands, and she provides empathy and a willingness to be there for me. I have an excellent psychiatrist, and he has provided the medical answers more than once during sustained bouts. I have friends who know me and accept me for who I am.

I know personally that physical pain can also contribute to suffering.

I suffer from the nagging pain that comes with osteoarthritis. Yes, it hurts, but do I suffer from it? No, I do not suffer. I have experienced debilitating pain. This level ten out of ten pain was so excruciating as to cause me to scream in agony and get physically sick to my stomach. It was relieved with a successful diagnosis and surgery. Thankfully my physical pain, unlike emotional pain, has not been as chronic. I have been able to cope better emotionally because of my relationship with Jesus Christ. AA provides relief through a spiritual program of fellowship and its Twelve Steps. I have a fabulous support group that includes a loving wife and family and numerous AA friends. Having said that, I have not always suffered well. Some people seem to respond to suffering with more acceptance and less whining.

My sister Jill is a perfect example. My younger sister, Barb, and I referred to Jill while she was alive as "St. Jill." Her faith was rock-solid. She had always been a very religious person, and she relied on her personal connection with Jesus to get her through difficult times. When queried about her source of solace, she would just smile and say something like "I just know Jesus will take care of me." She lost her hair from Propecia at an early age. It never seemed to bother her. I can recall the times when she would sit with her wig askance and would laugh out loud if someone told her to look at herself in the mirror. She developed heart disease. I remember one trip she made to California, where we were living at the time. We were walking on a path on Catalina Island, and she could not go twenty feet without having to stop and catch her breath. It did not get better for her. She had several surgeries without success. One visit to the hospital after an episode led her to consider a heart transplant. She opted for another solution that was a new procedure at the time. It was a miraculous device that could be surgically installed called a "heart pump." At night it could be connected to a power source. During the day, she wore a vest that stored several large batteries that weighed her down, but at least it permitted some mobility. She never complained. She would just smile and proclaim, "At least I will get to be with my grandchildren." She lived another eight years until a fainting episode put her back in the hospital, where the only option left was a heart transplant. Because there were too many antibodies from previous surgeries, she was rejected as a candidate. She took it all with a level of an acceptance I would not have been able to muster. She limped on for a while and eventually her heart condition caused strokes that put her in the hospital for the final time.

The family was called to be at her side in intensive care and Jill could not communicate due to the respirator she needed to keep her alive. Her only means of communication was to wiggle her right foot slightly to respond to questions. After several days with no progress, the palliative care physician told the family that there would be no recovery. The decision was made to cease respiration, and seconds later, she mercifully left this realm. Did she suffer? Despite all the medication to ease her pain, I suspect she did. Did she surrender to the suffering? No, in my observation, she did not. She displayed a dignity and strength to the very end. She really was St. Jill, and she is an example for me even now. She demonstrated without reservation that it is possible to suffer but not be overwhelmed by it. How did she do it? Her faith was the only logical explanation. Like the Buddha, she somehow was able to look at it, see the deeper lesson from it, and then she chose to respond in a way that transformed it into peace, joy, and liberation.

After reading and referencing numerous writings on Buddhism, I can see why so many people practice it. Some approach it as a religion; others to cope with suffering. It is the latter approach that I will pursue. I am a Christian. I believe that Jesus Christ is the Son of God. The Buddha is not God, nor will I ever worship as a Buddhist. However, I will keep an open mind as I consider Buddhism and its practice.

The key parts Buddhism can be summed up with the four noble truths and the noble eightfold path.

The Four Noble Truths

There are four noble truths in Buddhism.

1. Suffering exists. People invariably have had to endure physical suffering. The world and all humans living in it are imperfect. There is sickness, injury, old age, and ultimately death. We will never be able to keep all that we strive for.

2. Suffering arises from attachment to desires. This may include things like cravings for pleasure or wishes for fame and financial success. These kinds of things create suffering because loss is going to occur eventually.

3. Suffering ceases when attachment to desire ceases. It is the liberation of suffering. It is freedom from all worries, troubles, and harmful thought. This liberation is sometimes referred to as enlightenment.

4. Freedom from suffering is possible by practicing the eightfold path.

The Noble Eightfold Path

There are eight things that must be followed on the path to find freedom from suffering. Buddhists say that if we follow these eight paths, we can end the craving and desire that cause suffering and disappointment in life. I have been told that they are not to be followed sequentially, but while interdependent, they can be practiced individually.

1. right view
2. right intention
3. right speech
4. right action
5. right livelihood
6. right effort
7. right mindfulness
8. right concentration

I am hopeful that the eightfold path will offer a relief from suffering and provide another way to grow intellectually, emotionally, and spiritually.

1. Right View

This is where the path begins but also ends. It has been called the cognitive aspect of wisdom. It is more than just an intellectual awareness.

It will be achieved by using all aspects of my mind. My AA program also teaches that all actions are preceded by thoughts. I must have right thought if I am to obtain right behavior. It also means to see and to understand things as they really are. Isn't this the definition of insight? Dr. Phil defines insight as "the ability to see and understand why you do the things you do. The ability to see yourself without distortion."

Buddhists would add that it will enable the practitioner to see things through and to grasp the impermanent and imperfect nature of worldly objects and ideas. *Right view* begins with the insight that life means suffering and ends with complete understanding of the true nature of all things.

2. Right Intention

Are my intentions honorable? I have heard that the road to Hades is paved with good intentions. The need for right intention suggests there must be more than just having a right goal, but in addition, my motives had better match my intentions. Right intention also means that there must be a genuine commitment to thinking and behaving better. To be rightly intentional suggests to me that this is more than just being accountable for my actions. I must be focused on both ethical and mental self-improvement. The Buddha distinguishes the following three types of right intentions:

> ➤ the intention of renunciation, which means resistance to the pull of desire
> ➤ the intention of good will, meaning resistance to feelings of anger and aversion
> ➤ the intention of harmlessness, meaning not to act cruelly, violently, or aggressively, and to develop compassion

Not only will I desire to do the next right thing as AA suggests, but I will also try to do this free of as many of my defects of character as possible. I personally will have to lean into my inventory work to be freed from *the intention of renunciation* and the *intention of good will.* My first book, *Spiritual Awakening,* describes my journey to be delivered from the addictions of alcohol, work, shopping, and lust. I have made significant progress, but I claim spiritual progress, not spiritual perfection.

3. Right Speech

The words I choose can make a difference in how I am perceived. People react to what I say and how I say it. I must choose words that match my intention for ethical conduct, because ethical conduct is a guideline to moral discipline. My speech during AA meetings has not always matched my intentions for ethical conduct. I hear others who swear during meetings, mostly newcomers who use profanity, and colorful language is used to add emphasis. I swore during meetings at times myself, I'm guessing, to gain "street creds." I thought I needed to swear to appear more acceptable to those who also swore. I now know that I was not being true to my goal of becoming more like Christ. I was sinking to the level of the room rather than elevating my speech to a higher standard. Why do I ever swear? It is usually because I am letting my emotions override my ethics. I let my emotions control me. I swear when I am afraid, angry, and resentful. I am out of control.

I should know better. As a child, I remember taking a pledge provided by my piano teacher, who was a member of the LTL (Loyal Temperance Legion). It went something like "From alcohol and tobacco I'll abstain, and never take the Lord's name in vain." The Buddha would have been proud of her, but he would expand the list. He would ask me

> - to abstain from false speech, especially not to tell deliberate lies and not to speak deceitfully
> - to abstain from slanderous speech and not to use words maliciously against others
> - to abstain from harsh words that offend of hurt others
> - to abstain from idle chatter that lacks purpose of depth

I interpret this as telling the truth, being kind to others taking care to not offend or hurt others, and in general keeping my conversations to a minimum by talking less rather than more. When I do talk, I should have something worthwhile to say, avoiding gossip. And as my mother told me as a child, if I do not have anything nice to say, say nothing at all. *Is it necessary? Is it true? Is it kind?* If I cannot answer all three questions in the affirmative, I had better adjust my dialogue or perhaps say nothing.

Even my facial expressions and body language reactions can betray my ethical intentions This certainly adds another deeper dimension to *live and let live*, and furthermore, it gives me guidance on the types of speech from which I should abstain.

4. Right Action

I must avoid actions that will harm myself or others. My actions must be wholesome. Wholesome actions lead to a sound state of mind. In general, right action implies abstinence. I can relate to that as AA suggests total abstinence from drugs and alcohol, but the abstinence doesn't stop there. I must

> ▸ avoid harming "sentient beings, (beings with consciousness)" especially murder or suicide
> ▸ avoid intentional harm of any kind
> ▸ abstain from taking what is not given, including stealing, robbery, fraud, deceitfulness, and dishonesty
> ▸ abstain from sexual misconduct and assuring those sexual relationships do not harm anyone

The Bible suggests additional behaviors that must be eliminated.

> But now you must also rid yourselves of all such things as these: anger, rage, malice, slander, and filthy language from your lips. (Colossians 3:8 NIV)

Right action means not only ridding myself of negative behavior but also behaving productively, packing all that is right and good into the stream of life. My interactions with others are to reflect kindness and compassion without doing anything that might harm myself or others. My actions should reflect the best version of myself. I not only need to *talk the talk*, but I will also need to *walk the walk*.

5. Right Livelihood

This means that one's method of earning should be legal and not harmful to others. The Buddha mentions the following four specific types of work that should be avoided:

> dealing in weapons
> dealing in living beings, including prostitution and slave trade; it also should not include raising animals that will be slaughtered (i.e., meat production and butchery)
> selling intoxicants and poisons, such as drugs and alcohol
> any occupation that would violate the principles of right speech and right actions

The underlying theme implies that my livelihood must do no harm to any living animal. That begs the question as to what the Buddha's stance would be on harming the environment. I'm guessing that it would fall under the category of not harming any living being. I must not harm myself or any other living being. Sounds like I should live and let live. Having just been bombarded by a contentious election, I wonder what the Buddha's stance would be on the occupation of politician. I'm leaning toward the notion that if we would follow the eightfold path, we wouldn't need them.

While I understand the Buddha's underlying intent for selecting a livelihood, I feel like there is another element to consider. Is my contribution useful? If I am not adding to the stream of life in a positive way, and if I do not really love what I am doing, then I am likely not contributing positively.

6. Right Effort

This includes willful actions that are driven by wholesome states of mind. Again, right thinking begets right action. Negative states of mental energy will fuel desire, envy, aggression, and violence. Positive states of mental energy can drive right efforts like self-discipline, honesty, benevolence, and kindness. Buddha describes four types of endeavors that rank in ascending order of perfection:

> to prevent the arising of un-arisen unwholesome states
> to abandon unwholesome states that have already arisen
> to arouse wholesome states that have not yet arisen
> to maintain and perfect wholesome states already arisen

I would interpret the goal of these endeavors is to rid myself of things that feed and grow my lower self and strive for things that feed and grow my higher self.

7. Right Mindfulness

Right mindfulness is the mental ability to see things as they are with clear consciousness. It requires honest and unbiased interpretation of stimuli. It is common to interpret events and stimuli with half consciousness, and as a result, the things we see become obscured. Right mindfulness would enable me to be aware of the process of conceptualization in a way that I can observe and control the way my thoughts go. Buddha described the following as the four foundations of mindfulness:

> contemplation of the body
> contemplation of feeling (repulsive, attractive, or neutral)
> contemplation of the state of mind
> contemplation of the phenomena

Mindfulness will be explored in more detail later in the Seven Factors of Awakening. My goal is to be able to respond to all stimuli with an honest and accurate assessment of what truly is. My problem in the past was to rely on conditioned responses that were not always based in truth. My assessments were, and often still are, distorted and biased.

8. Right Concentration

The simple definition of right concentration is a state where all mental faculties are unified and directed onto one object. It is wholesome concentration on thoughts and actions. Buddhists achieve this through the practice of meditation. The meditating mind focuses on a selected object in step-by-step levels of concentration. Through practice, it becomes natural to apply elevated levels of concentration in everyday situations.

There are additional details of Buddhism that devout practitioners find important. There is a lot to consider. I found that Thich Nhat Hahn's book *The Heart of the Buddha's Teaching* was very helpful as an overview to the Buddhist practice. There is a lot to learn that goes well beyond what I have explored so far, such as the two truths, the three Dharma seals, the three jewels, the four immeasurable minds, the five aggregates, the five powers, the six paramitas, the seven factors of awakening, the links of interdependent co-arising, and touching the Buddha within. The book is an insightful and revealing introduction to Buddhism.

Regarding the study of Buddhism, I am curious about the totality of what might be required of me. However, I am less interested in the dogma and liturgy than I am in its practicality. The part of the practice that seems most applicable to me will focus on the factors that will permit more growth into my own personal spiritual awakening.

The Seven Factors of Awakening

The Seven Factors of Awakening are mindfulness, investigation of phenomena, diligence, joy, ease, concentration, and letting go. I have been told that awakening can also be referred to as enlightenment. What a blessed destination that could be.

Since the twelfth step of my AA program also suggests a "spiritual" awakening can be achieved by working the Twelve Steps, I see parallels between AA's Twelve Steps and how the Seven Factors of Awakening could contribute to my spiritual growth.

Mindfulness

The Buddha promises realization of the Seven Factors of Awakening if the four establishments of mindfulness are practiced. This appears to be preparatory in nature. This is the one-way path for the purification of beings, for the surmounting of sorrow and lamentations, for the passing away of pain and dejection, for the attainment of the true way, for the realization of Nibbana—namely, the four establishments of mindfulness.

I would have to consider my physical being, emotions, rational thoughts, and observations in a totally focused and open-minded receptive way—curious and searching, without prejudice. Mindfulness requires an honest, focused, and intentional connection with everything that I do and comprehend in relationship to my surroundings. I must become aware of who I am, where I am, who I am with, and what I am doing. I am to be totally cognizant of myself in my surroundings but free from any distraction that might diminish the truth in that experience. The difficult task in attaining mindfulness is staying true to what I am sensing. This requires ignoring the distracting thoughts that take me away from focusing solely on my steps, my breath, and the things around me.

If I happen to walk by a dry cleaner and start thinking that I need to pick up my cleaning, I am no longer focusing on my steps, my breath, or the phenomena around me. It isn't until I start focusing again on my breathing or feel my feet hitting the pavement that I can return to mindfulness. My journey is to see things the way they really are without any personal valuation of good or bad. Like the AA program, it will require "rigorous honesty." I must accept things the way they truly are, and from that admission, I begin to seek humility and awakening.

Mindfulness allows freedom from the material world and thereby leads to freedom from want, freedom from fear, and ultimately *freedom from suffering*. Freedom from the material world goes against my natural inclinations. I have spent a lifetime trying to fit in with the material world. Now am I to cast off everything I have felt and thought for a lifetime? Am I to wear the world like a loose garment, like I have heard from those more spiritually evolved than I? And what does that really mean anyway? Should I start buying clothes a size larger? If I remain in that lower level of thinking, I may be either rebelling against the inevitable truth that I have been unable to face up until now or just making something more difficult than it needs to be.

The awareness may become a little clearer if I consider the term *to fit in*. From the early elementary school days on the playground, I was found anxiously waiting to be selected by the captain on one of two teams. I was hearing the names being called out one by one. As the names were called out, my confidence and self-worth diminished with every name that was not my own. I must admit I still feel like that today during AA meetings using the "tag" method, where people who have shared get to arbitrarily pick the next person to share. If I'm not selected to share, why do I still feel unwanted? Clearly, I was codependent back then, and like Bill Wilson, I still need approval and acceptance to a fault.

If I look at the two words from which the word mindful is derived, *mind* and *full,* I can literally evaluate what fills my mind. Whatever I think about eventually drives how I feel and what I will do. If I keep dredging up unpleasant events from the past, I will likely suffer from resentment. If I worry for future events that haven't yet happened, I will waste the life I have right now. What remains is the present. I am to be totally aware of where I am and what I am doing. Once I am "present," I can accept my current reality and respond rationally with less emotional distraction.

Investigation of Phenomena

This investigation is different from what a detective might do when he or she investigates a crime scene. That kind of investigation may be conducted to support a particular suspicion or to try to prove a preconceived outcome. The investigators will use the facts to support a claim of innocence or proof of guilt. This kind of investigation comes from a truly willing and open mind to let things reveal themselves. Without this honest search, I will eventually go back to my well of bad habits and ideas. That will lead to practicing my shortcomings and ultimately a relapse to my lower self.

In the morning from my deck, I stare out at the golf course adjacent to my home. There is a berm with bushes and small trees that run parallel to the cart path that runs just behind my house. I often watch the golfers stop their carts near that berm and then start their search for a golf ball that may have made its way into my garden. I am not looking for anything, and this would not qualify as the type of "investigation of phenomena" the Buddha may have had in mind.

But what if I diverted my attention to the bushes where I spotted a small bud that had appeared on one of the trees? It had just bloomed on one of the branches, and as I stared, I might say something like "Where did you come from, and where will you go? Your bud will transform into a flower or perhaps a leaf. Will you always be small and green?" The bud might respond with "I may start small, but I will grow. I will change forms and ultimately wither and die and fall from the bush to become part of the earth. The earth is quite large, so will I be as large as the earth?"

My first reaction to what I just wrote is to question the sanity of talking to buds. My apologies for any pedestrian thought, but it recalls a Disney movie featuring a song called "Zip-a-Dee-Doo-Dah." During one of the scenes in the movie, the singer is joined by numerous animations of birds and animals joyously encouraging the singer's message. Fantasy, unadulterated fantasy that would not meet today's woke standards for racial justice, but back then it was joyfully entertaining.

Now after further consideration and with a bit more open mind, I will try to think of the message behind my word picture. For me, it is an allegory for change. We are in a state of constant flux. In this realm, what appears to be small can grow to something very large. There is an impermanence to the things around us. From the earth, the plant emerged, and to the earth, the plant returned. The plant we see is temporal, but the process of change is eternal.

> By the sweat of your brow you will eat your food until you return to the ground, since from it you were taken; for dust you are and to dust you will return. (Genesis 3:19 NIV)

This insight does not diminish my worth of existence but reveals my true part in the whole of existence. I am neither better nor worse in any hierarchy of life, but I just am. Successful investigation of the phenomena around me finally frees me from the bondage of self. I truly am finally able to wear the world like a loose garment. I can comfortably seek humility and enable a focus on the needs of others.

Diligence

If one is true to one's practice and remains diligent, one will be rewarded with energy. I compare it to the experience of exercise. I know that there will be a certain amount of pain during the exercise, but I know that it will result in being more physically fit and that will give me energy. The pain from exercise is worth it because I get the benefits of strength, health, and energy. But what about emotional pain or spiritual pain? Even then my life has meaning.

Before retirement, I was a diligent worker. In fact, I was more than diligent. I was addicted. I was a workaholic. My profession as a consultant permitted plenty of opportunities to be a part of a solution as I worked with clients. There were times when I felt I was indeed making a difference. When I felt that way, the experience was energizing. I was diligent—not so much out of a sense of duty but more from the awareness that my contribution was sincerely appreciated. There were times when it truly brought *meaning to my life*.

I recently sat in a meeting and listened to an alcoholic with thirty-five years of sobriety recount his day. His message was directed intentionally to another alcoholic who was suffering from loneliness. He started his share, describing his routine of getting up early and getting things done. He had tended to his garden and then set about repairing and repainting a picnic table. His wife came out on the patio much later in the day. Unlike him, she stays up late every night and gets up much later the next morning. The first words out of her mouth had to do with what she had heard from a politician she was watching on network TV. She was upset by what the politician said and the dialogue with her husband evolved into a disagreement and eventually changed the mood for them both.

The storyteller's intent was to let the lonely alcoholic know that there are times when being lonely isn't so bad. There was much laughter as many of the attendees could identify with that experience. Thinking back on the circumstances that the alcoholic shared, I have another awareness that ties to the factor of diligence. The alcoholic was energized by his diligence to the tasks he completed, and he was happy with what he accomplished. His life had meaning. His wife, on the other hand, chose to sleep late, watch TV, and was contentious and therefore did not earn the benefits of diligence.

I can confirm that I am energized when I am diligent with my prayer and meditation time as well as my service work. My life has meaning. I cannot grow spiritually, and I will not be useful, unless I am diligent. Yet diligence requires discipline. The chapter "Into Action" from the Big Book of Alcoholics Anonymous describes alcoholics as undisciplined and suggests that we use the steps, particularly steps ten and eleven, to let God discipline us. So more than just a means to sobriety, I will let the steps discipline me to diligence.

Ease

Most of my problems are of my own making. I keep falling back into the belief that if I just apply myself better, I can prevail. I had a career that required my ability to problem-solve. I applied my problem-solving and communication skills and abilities successfully and achieved the goals I set for my clients and myself.

In retirement, the skills and abilities that worked so well in my work career no longer work as well. Why? Perhaps it is the way I viewed my work. I would tell everybody that I really enjoyed the challenge of my work. There was a great deal of satisfaction in completing project after project successfully. I now accept that stress was a necessary occupational hazard that came with the work.

Today I do not have the work-related stress. Today the challenges inherent to the work are gone, so why do I still feel stress? In my first book, *Spiritual Awakening*, I chronicled how the work itself ironically permitted a distraction from the outcomes of stress. I became addicted to work even after the compulsion to drink had been removed. I may have accepted stress as a by-product of my work addiction similarly to accepting the hangovers I endured because of my alcohol addiction.

Today I no longer desire to accept stress as a necessary by-product of my retirement. So why do I keep flogging myself with it? Maybe I'm overly sensitive to the events of the world around me. There seems to be plenty of explanation for why stress is so pervasive. Recent times have been stressful—a presidential election, and a COVID-19 pandemic to name a couple. There are those that would abandon capitalism and replace it with socialism. Even so, does it really mean that times are more stressful today than they ever were? Every period in history could likely report stressful times. The question remains: how do I deal with stress?

The ease with which I respond to stress is up to me to determine. I must take time today, particularly that I no longer have the distraction of work, to be sure I am *diligent* in my routine of relaxation, prayer, and meditation. My AA program has slogans that suggest a reaction of "Easy does it" or "Let go and let God." Someone else reminded me, "Nothing too good or too bad lasts too long." The Bible advises that worry cannot add even one hour to my life. The Serenity Prayer starts with "God, grant me the serenity ..." The first word of the prayer is "God." God grants me serenity. It is a gift given *prior* to any ability I may ever have to accept the things I cannot change. Most everything will be unacceptable to me if I do not surrender to God. Acceptance comes from God!

I cannot control what happens in the world, but I can affect how I react to what happens in the world. Like a song by the Eagles suggests, I want a "peaceful, easy feeling." The lyrics for the chorus ending with "Cause I'm already standin' *on the ground*" remind me of a Bible verse that one translation suggests that I "be still." I will need to stop or desist my feeble attempts to control things I cannot control. I will need to cease fighting anything or anybody. I must cease stiving. I am a "human being" and not a "human doing." I must bow to the one true God and exalt him forever.

> He says, "Be still, and know that I am God; I will be exalted among the nations, I will be exalted in the earth." (Psalm 46:10 NIV)

Literally and spiritually, I need to be grounded. This relationship I'm growing with "God of my understanding" keeps me grounded, and I *will* know peace if I remain *diligent*.

Joy

During the COVID-19 pandemic, many AA in-person meetings were restricted to no more than ten persons, along with numerous other limitations. Weather permitting, many of these meetings moved to outdoor locations. During one of those meetings held in a large park, as people were sharing, I noticed several children running back and forth across a large, grassy area of the park. There was no apparent motivation to this random movement other than the fact that they enjoyed it for its own sake. I was too far away to see all their expressions, but I could tell from their body language that they were experiencing joy.

In that same park, I saw a mother pushing a stroller with a small child. What was most noticeable was the child's expressions. And what was most prominent were the eyes. They were wide open, intent, and focused. The eyes spoke to the awe that emanated from their reaction. The child seemed filled with joy for each new scene as the mom pushed the child through the trees into the open field.

Joy seems to emanate more naturally from children. Years of stress, disappointment, unfulfilled dreams, disease, and the like take a toll on many. But is it still possible to experience joy?

My program suggests that the joy of living is the theme behind AA's Twelve Steps. The AA program wants us all to be happy, joyous, and free. Our crowd absolutely insists on enjoying life, and so does my Heavenly Father.

> Until now you have not asked for anything in my name. Ask and you will receive, and your joy will be complete. (John 16:24 NIV)

There was a song I recall singing early on in Sunday school. It included hand and body movements that went with the lyrics.

> I've got the joy, joy, joy, joy
> Down in my heart (where?)
> Down in my heart (where?)
> Down in my heart
> I've got the joy, joy, joy, joy

Down in my heart (where?)
Down in my heart to stay. (Lyrics by George William Cook)

I remember singing the song as loudly as I could sing. Other children didn't sing but shouted the words and danced and twirled with abandon. They ignored the choreography; they responded naturally as they were moved by the music. They really meant it. I really meant it. There was no doubt as to the authenticity and depth of our feeling. I wish I could recapture that level of faith and joy. I am at times able to replicate a reasonable facsimile but only if my heart and mind are receptive. I cherish those memories. I look forward to the time when there will be ceaseless joy without end in heaven. It warms my heart to think about it. I feel joyous in anticipation. Come, Lord Jesus. Come.

Concentration

Even in the moments requiring complete focus, my mind often wanders. Like anything worth doing well, I should be willing to concentrate well. After all, didn't God give us our minds to use? Mindfulness, once developed, permits concentration. I desire to concentrate more effectively, particularly during prayer.

Isn't prayer a form of concentration? After all, the prayer emanates from my mind. If I am praying that God directs His mercy, forgiveness, or blessing to people or individuals, isn't it because I acknowledge that God is the source of the power? My brain connects with the energy that my Higher Power provides and because of my focus, the energy is then directed to me. Perhaps this is why people rely on the "power" of prayer. It also explains why many who pray say that quantity matters. The number of folks praying seems to amplify the effect. Therefore, church congregations and prayer groups pray together. My old church asked the congregants for prayer requests so that they can be offered up during congregation prayer time.

I can think of another example of how this form of concentration has been applied. During medical procedures that I have had, where there will be a short period of discomfort or perhaps pain, I have heard the practitioner tell me to not hold my breath but to breathe steadily and focus my mind on the area where the pain may emanate. I am told to direct my thoughts to that spot with a warm, comforting energy and breathe into the painful area. Amazingly, the pain is not as intense. Is it just a distraction, or does the breath itself have the power to alleviate the pain? Didn't it all start with breath?

> Then the LORD God formed a man from the dust of the ground and breathed into his nostrils the breath of life, and the man became a living being. (Genesis 2:7 NIV)

Can this power of concentration can be used to escape the pain and suffering of this world? Could this literally be true? Apparently, the Buddha was able to use concentration and meditation to remove himself from the world, but he decided that it was not useful because it did nothing to alleviate suffering.

I have a friend who was at the bedside of his sponsor who lay dying. The sponsor's words were eerily profound. He looked into my friend's eyes and said, "Pay attention!" That was all he said. My friend later wondered where he should direct his attention. I now think I know what his sponsor meant. He was entreating his sponsee to avoid meaningless distractions, to pay attention, to focus, and to be mindful— to *concentrate!*

Letting Go

Letting go seems to be the goal of all the seven aspects of awakening. If I can practice the previous aspects with diligence and consistency, I will have come a long way in my search for emotional sobriety and integrity. I will come closer to achieving the goal implied by the title of this book, *Live and Let Live.*

Jesus said, "I came that they might have life and have it abundantly" (John 10:10 EST). The message is clear throughout the New Testament. If I accept Jesus into my life and believe that He died for my sins, I will not die but have everlasting life. I will be transformed. I will live less for myself and more for the opportunities to do God's will, which will include a life of service and caring for the needs of others.

The Buddha speaks of this in a similar way. He describes it as equanimity.

I am to be loving and tolerant. "Love and tolerance of others is our code." Additionally, the underlying principle of all the Twelve Steps of AA is humility. Eventually I will achieve humility to the extent that I admit "I can't, but God can." That leads to another AA suggestion. "Let go and let God."

The Bible tells me to "turn the other cheek" when slapped and that I should love others as I love myself. My observation of the world's actions today is that these suggestions are rarely followed. This, like a lot of the suggestions in the Bible and the Big Book of Alcoholics Anonymous, seems impossible for humans to achieve. What should I do if I am shopping in a downtown area of a large city and suddenly accosted by an angry mob of protesters? They are armed with bricks and commercial grade fireworks and have looted, set fires to businesses, and torn down historical statues that they found offensive. They fearlessly proclaim that they want to burn down our current system of governance so that they can replace it with one that is better. This is happening in a large urban city. Is this the will of a small group of protesters or a placeholder for the will of large numbers of citizens?

The country seems divided on how to react to this and similar events. One voice would have the government send in federal law enforcement to protect property and restore law. Another voice tells the police to stand down in the face of riots and then works to defund their budget. They want to empty jails and eliminate laws and culture that they say are mired in institutional racism. They want numerous categories of folks and institutions to admit and eliminate their "white privilege." They want to cancel a culture and history they think is racist. They want a redistribution of wealth and reparations. They want to replace equality with equity. So who's right? Is there another option? What would the Buddha suggest? I should *practice equanimity.*

If I am successful in practicing and achieving all seven of the aspects of awakening, will I have an awakening like the kind of awakening that came from the completion of the first eleven steps of the AA program? Is this achievement the same as what the Buddhists call enlightenment? I think it is.

While I am intrigued by the teachings of the Buddha, I lack any firsthand experience. To get an explanation from one who practices Buddhist philosophy, I went to a friend in AA to learn more.

She was drawn to Buddhism not as religion but to enhance her spiritual growth. She attends a Sri Lanka temple and does engage in the rituals but less for the dogma and more out of respect and personal interest. She went primarily for the meditation and to learn how her mind works. She said she learned about four types of meditation: walking, standing, lying, and sitting. Also, there are six sense doors in Buddhist philosophy: eyes, ears, taste, touch, body, and mind. When sitting in front of the altar with the Buddha and incense, she focuses first on her body and then on her breath. She becomes an observer of phenomena. She notices the ambient sounds, smells, tastes, etc. and then "sees" her emotions. This sounds like Vipassana, which is a Buddhist guided meditation that starts at one end of the body and observes sensations at every point until the other end is reached.

When there is a thought, my friend "lets it go." Prior to her practice, she admitted to having a very ruminating mind. It was always going. She now says that her mind has become "increasingly quiet." She is now able to catch her thoughts and not be hooked on them. She is learning not to be driven by thoughts and emotions. Isn't that my goal for emotional sobriety? During this process of sitting on a cushion for thirty to forty-five minutes, she has learned to quiet her mind and emotions. She reported that it carries over to day-to-day activities and she can attain what seems like a "quiet muscle memory" to skillfully respond. She is learning to cultivate the wholesome and abandon the unwholesome. She is learning to engage the world skillfully. She is seeing things the way they really are while unlearning her old, conditioned responses.

Isn't this like what the practitioners of emotional intelligence are trying to achieve? By living without prejudices, biases, and expectations, she is better able to move on to do the next right thing. She is therefore much less reactionary and less likely to take the actions of others personally.

If a person desires to live and let live, the tenets of Buddhist philosophy are reasonable. Anyone trying to achieve emotional sobriety would certainly be willing to practice the Five Precepts of Buddhism:

> no killing: respect for life
> no stealing: respect for others' property
> no sexual misconduct: respect for our pure nature
> no lying: respect for honesty
> no intoxicants: respect for a clear mind

Are Teachings of Buddha Similar to Teachings of Jesus?

I heard someone at a meeting say that Jesus was a Buddhist. I believe that Jesus came into the world as the Son of God. He wasn't a Buddhist in the religious sense, but He did preach similar ways to live more fully. And like Buddhism, His teachings seem irrefutable as an ideal, although unlikely to be followed by many. There have been exceptions. I can recall a time in our history that there were those who behaved as though they believed in something similar.

Martin Luther King Jr. is a person who comes to mind. He preached nonviolence yet strongly upheld the principles of the change he espoused. He preached about a time when people of all colors could be united and live freely together without prejudice or bias.

Abraham Lincoln is another example, and while his solution included a Civil War that cost 700,000 lives, he never wavered from his belief that all people are created equal.

John Kennedy famously said, "Ask not what your country can do for you, but what you can do for your country."

Jesus preached nonviolence and hung out with tax collectors and heathens. He recognized the condition of the world and wore it like a loose garment. He preached love yet suggested that we coexist in the world.

> "Tell us then, what is your opinion? Is it right to pay the imperial tax to Caesar or not?"
>
> But Jesus, knowing their evil intent, said, "You hypocrites, why are you trying to trap me?
>
> Show me the coin used for paying the tax." They brought him a denarius, and he asked them, "Whose image is this? And whose inscription?"

*"Caesar's," they replied. Then he said to them, "So give
back to Caesar what is Caesar's, and to God what is God's."
(Matthew 22:17–21 NIV)*

What do these people have in common besides a dream for a better
life? They were not afraid to go against popular belief. They challenged
mainstream thinking. They were passionate and consistent with their
message. Sadly, they were all murdered because of their beliefs. That is
an important consideration as I face the path to awakening. There is a
lingering suspicion that if I follow a similar path of what the Buddha
and these martyrs have done, at least it will not always be easy, and at
the worst, there will be opposition, possibly with violence by those with
selfish motives and opposing views.

Bottom line is the choice must be made. Would I be willing to
die to defend my beliefs? Am I willing to commit to and strive for a
deeper awakening? Will I have the courage to do what is necessary to
overcome all obstacles? Do I really aspire to become more useful for
God's purpose? As the AA Big Book suggests, am I willing to go to any
length? Or am I to slip back into the crowd and settle for the "easier,
softer way" and never become the best version of myself? I pray for
God's guidance and strength. I desire to do God's will.

Prayer. What are prayer and meditation? What are the distinctions
between the two? Prayer may be considered our attempt to talk to God,
and meditation is our effort to listen. Prayer is a necessary part of what
I do every day to connect with my Higher Power, whom I choose to call
God. I also believe that I must pray to have a stronger faith. Faith leads
to prayer and prayer leads to faith.

What do I pray for? I pray for guidance. I ask God to direct my
thinking. I ask God to remove any character defects that stand in the
way of my usefulness to God and the people I meet. I pray for knowledge
of God's will for me and the power to carry that out. I pray to give God
thanks for all the blessings He has provided and for His solutions to my
problems. I pray for God's will to be done for friends and family. I make
specific requests for their health and well being, but I try not to pray
for specific outcomes for myself unless it will help others. I pray for the
glorification of God's kingdom.

I try to pray throughout the day, as this is the way I remain in conscious contact. I pray for intuitive thoughts and guidance. I pray to be relieved from temptation, anxiety, and fear.

Sometimes the prayers are short and repeated like a mantra or even a meditation. I say, "God, help me," and repeat it often. Sometimes I pray, "Come, Holy Spirit. Come." And again, I repeat it. If I am trying to communicate effectively or help others, I may ask directly with something like "Please give me the words to say" or "Please help me to be useful." I pray for God's mercy and intervention for the needs of my country and the world. Like those in previous generations who despaired at the condition of their circumstances, I pray, "Kyrie Eleison. Christi Eleison" or "Lord have mercy, Christ have mercy." I may pray something like "All praise and honor and glory to You, oh God!" I pray to acknowledge my joy and gratitude. It's my prayer of praise and joy for my connection with God. I gratefully pray for all the blessings God has provided.

A good friend in AA has shared that one of the shortest prayers is nothing more than the one-word prayer of "Thank You." Sometimes I acknowledge my humility, that of myself I am nothing but with God I am everything. I may pray something like "You are the source of my power and strength, oh God."

I may repeat the Serenity Prayer. "God grant me the serenity to accept the things I cannot change, the courage to change the things that I can, and the wisdom to know the difference." I have found that I rely on this prayer for more than just the beginning and end of an AA meeting but as a cry for help when I am in need.

Jesus taught His disciples to pray something like this: "My Father, Holy is Your name. Your kingdom come; your will be done on earth as it is in heaven. Give me today my daily food and forgive my sins as I forgive the sins of others. Rescue me from temptation and deliver me from evil. For the kingdom and power and glory are Yours, now and forever. Amen."

When I continue to pray this prayer daily, it means that I am now willing to rely on God for everything. I acknowledge that He alone is supreme and holy. I pray that God's will be done in this realm just as it is being done in heaven. I am asking for what is necessary for daily survival. I acknowledge my sins, and I am asking for forgiveness just as I pray for the willingness to forgive others for any harm that they have done to me. I pray that I will be rescued from temptation and be delivered from evil. I acknowledge that God is in charge and all power comes from Him. I acknowledge His omnipotence and give Him all the glory now and for all eternity.

I pray first thing in the morning on my knees to be shown throughout the day what God would have me to be and do. I ask God to direct my thinking and direct me away from selfishness and more toward what I can do for others. I ask to be delivered from dishonesty, resentment, and fear. My prayer includes segments from various prayers included in the AA Big Book that are suggested for steps three, seven, ten, and eleven. I do not pray them verbatim, but as a friend in AA shares, "I pray my own versions." Some of the portions of those prayers may include the following:

> God, I offer myself to You, to build with me and do with me as You will.
> Relieve me of the bondage of self that I may better do Your will.
> Take away my difficulties that victory over them may bear witness to Your power, Your love, and Your way of life.
> Heavenly Father, I am now willing that You should have all of me, good and bad.
> Remove any defects of character that may stand in the way of my usefulness to You and my fellows.
> This is a sick person. How can I be helpful? Please save me from being angry. Your will be done.
> Please help me to be tolerant and patient with others. Help me to bring good will to others, even my enemies. Help me to see them as sick people.
> God, I pray that I may be of maximum service to You and the people around me.
> My Creator, I am praying that You show me the way of patience, tolerance, kindliness, and love.
> God, please give me insight, inspiration, or an intuitive thought on what I should do next.

> God, I am praying for knowledge of Your will for me and the power to carry that out.

I pray for specific people, both in and out of the program. I end all prayers with "I ask for all of these things in Jesus's name. Amen." At night I pray the following:

> Thank You for keeping me sober.
> Thank You for all my blessings.
> Please forgive me for my shortcomings.
> Thank You, God, for Your protection and care.

I review my day and ask to be guided for recollection of where I may have been selfish, dishonest, resentful, or afraid. I ask for forgiveness and pray for guidance for the next right thing to do to better accomplish His will for me.

Meditation. Regarding prayer and meditation, when I am in over my head and do not know what to do, I pray for God's guidance; however, if I really want God's help, I need to meditate. I believe that meditation is the sincerest form of conscious contact I can have with God. I am indeed listening to God when I meditate. Meditation is the time I devote to listening for the Holy Spirit's guidance and comfort. I find that I must meditate if I am to receive AA's ninth step promise. "God is doing for me that I cannot do for myself."

Meditation is extremely practical. My attitude and behavior depend on *being ready* to receive God's assistance and guidance through the day. My experience over the years tells me that meditation works; it really does. I feel sorry for those who do not have the guidance of a power greater than themselves.

> I feel sorry for people that don't drink, because when they wake up in the morning, that is the best they are going to feel all day. (Frank Sinatra, Dean Martin, Sammy Davis Jr.)

Prior to meditation I relied on alcohol to alter my mood. Like other alcoholics, I woke up each morning and pursued whatever actions that popped into my head on a moment-to-moment basis. I may have prayed,

"God's will be done," but I behaved like it was "my will be done." I was satisfied with the results that come from self-reliance. I had not yet come to grips with the fact that I was suffering from the bondage of selfishness and fear. I now know that my disease will remain in remission one day at a time if I am in fit spiritual condition. I have the mind of an addict, and "self-centered fear" is enemy number one. I have heard fear described by a couple of acronyms. The first is false evidence appearing real; the second is future events already realized.

These potential manifestations are described further when I try to relieve myself of the bondage of fear. I am faced with what AA describes as a two-headed coin called "Ego." One side of the coin is "Pride," which says, "You need not pass this way," and the other side is "Fear," which says, "You dare not look." And if fear escalates to anger, it can get even worse. When that happens to me, I let the offenders live rent free in my head. Instead of communion with God, I have a tormented series of potentially false scenarios that cloud my thoughts and attitudes. I have little hope of receiving guidance from my God and my "lower self" will be running the show. That is no longer acceptable to me. I choose to improve my conscious contact with God as I understand Him. But just how am I to meditate?

There are numerous sites online and apps from most phone carriers' app stores that are available for a person to get started with meditation. Meditation helps me move from my head to my heart or gut. My sponsor used to say meditation helped him "get way down deep, where he lived." I use an app I purchased called Abide. It offers guided mediations based on Bible verses for various durations, anywhere from five minutes to fifteen minutes. Each daily meditation builds on a theme taken from a specific Bible verse. The speaker offers inspirational stories that fit the intended verse. The listener is asked to get comfortable and separate from any distractions. The listener is to then pray to have God remove any specific sins or shortcomings that may block a spiritual connection. We are then told to ask for forgiveness. The speaker then provides various versions of the scripture verse and asks the listener to reflect on their significance. The listener is asked to engage with the Holy Spirit to provide insight and direction on specific words or phrases the listener selects.

In addition to guided meditation, I have developed my own practice. I meditate most every morning and sometimes throughout the day. I am still practicing, but generally my meditation includes some of the following actions:

> I find a comfortable spot as free from distractions as possible.
> I take several deep, centering breaths. I focus entirely on my breathing.
> If my mind is racing to include other thoughts, I refocus on my breathing—nothing but the breath.
> I start to scan my body for any discomfort or pain that may distract and breathe into each of those locations.
> I relax any muscle tension that may distract and continue to breathe into any areas that may be painful.
> I relax my hands onto my lap and then into a palms-up receptive position.
> I continue to focus on my breathing, gently pulling away any unwanted thoughts that distract.
> As I inhale, I think, *God in*.
> As I exhale, I think, *Doug out*.
> As I inhale, I think, *Holy Spirit in*.
> As I exhale, I think, *Character defects out*.
> I focus on nothing but my breath.

As an alcoholic, I am told that I have a daily reprieve contingent on the maintenance of my spiritual condition. The time spent in meditation is quite practical. This *diligence* and *discipline* yield freedom from self and provide an uptick in mood and energy.

Concentration. In Buddhism, the eighth element of the Noble Path is *concentration*. I have a low-level ability to focus; perhaps it is a football game, or perhaps it is a conversation with my wife. Even under ideal conditions, I am often distracted and my attention gets diverted. I used to think I was able to think about more than one thing at a time. I now know that is impossible. If one or more distractions are present, my focus on the original object of my attention is lost or significantly diminished. I am slowly coming to understand that *listening intently* is highly important in relationships. The degree to which I listen is indicative of the value I place on the communicator or the message. It also is fundamental to the amount of knowledge I desire.

> Whoever has will be given more, and they will have an abundance. Whoever does not have, even what they have will be taken from them. (Matthew 12:12 NIV)

Buddhism defines right concentration as "wholesome concentration" and suggests concentration on wholesome thoughts and actions. The Buddhist method to develop right concentration is through the practice of meditation.

There are numerous ways that people have learned to meditate. One of the more popular methods is Transcendental Meditation . TM is a specific form of silent, mantra meditation created by Maharishi Mahesh Yogi TM technique and TM movement in India in the mid-1950s.

TM started more as a religion and moved to more of a scientific/ spiritual process to reduce stress. It became quite commercial and has grown to include online seminars and videos. It became popular with the rich and famous over the years and has been practiced by celebrities like the Beatles, Clint Eastwood, and Stevie Wonder. The Beatles traveled to India in 1968 and their training course in TM inspired them to give up drugs. There were additional trips to India, and it was George Harrison and John Lennon who remained the most faithful. Several songs evolved from this experience, including George Harrison's "The Inner Light" and John Lennon's "Across the Universe." There ended up being quite a bit of controversy eventually as the Maharishi was accused of becoming too commercial, using the Beatle's fame to promote TM.

8

Nirvana

Am I achieving what I hoped for on this personal journey for emotional sobriety? It started with a desire to achieve emotional sobriety that some equate to a spiritual awakening. That happened for me upon accomplishing the first eleven steps in the program of Alcoholics Anonymous. I am sober and most alcoholics never get sober. I truly am a miracle. Just like the first one hundred in AA, I have recovered from a hopeless state of mind and body. The thinking and behavior that once were ruled by my addiction are no more, at least regarding drinking and using. I still have defects of character and will never be defect free. I believe there is more than just trying to become a better person and to be satisfied with just doing the "next right thing." I want more than just to be free from the lash of alcohol.

I'm trying to fill the gap between that part of the twelfth step that says, "Having had a spiritual awakening," and the remainder of the step that says, "We tried to carry this message to alcoholics and practice these principles in all of our affairs." How can I sustain this effort with authenticity?

The Buddha said something along the lines that when there is wisdom, we can see the "the interbeing of all things." And while things may be "impermanent" in a physical sense, there is a spiritual feature of oneness that is genuinely transcendent. It takes us all beyond time and space and gets us into the realm of what always was and what always will be. What is nirvana? I have heard it described as a state that permits freedom from pain, worry, and the challenges of the external world.

The good news is I don't have to die to achieve nirvana. There just might be hope for "that peaceful easy feeling" right now by staying in the now. If I really live moment to moment and accept my reality with each breath I take, I can achieve nirvana.

Impermanence

If I just trust the process described, will I realize that I am not a physical entity having a spiritual experience but a spiritual entity living in a physical realm? Can impermanence, deeply touched, be eternal?

From my desk, I can see the angle created by my office door that is perpendicular to the wall where I can see the front door of my house. On one side, there are windows that were installed because the previous windows were starting to show their age. The new ones came with a long-wear warranty but are short of a lifetime guarantee. We replaced the front door to our home at the same time we replaced the windows. Looking through the office window, I see steps that were replaced because the cement was cracked and water collected every time it rained. When the water froze, it became a small skating rink. We replaced the front steps for cosmetic reasons in addition to drainage improvement. Unfortunately, the colors didn't turn out the way the contractor described. The stamped concrete was supposed to have a taupe cast with gray overtones. The result yielded a mottled green shade with splotches that looked like mold. My wife apologizes to visitors for the garish contrast. I look down past the steps to the driveway that was replaced due to cracking and crumbling cement. I was told that the concrete would be there thirty years from now. Does thirty years constitute a lifetime in cement durability? The driveway is filled with construction trucks. Workers are busy installing new cabinets in the kitchen. They are hauling cabinets across the foyer floor that will also be replaced. I was told that there will be a warranty on construction and labor. The old cabinets lasted thirty years. Will the new ones last that long? Looking past the trucks parked in my driveway, I see branches from our crabapple tree touching the dumpster that has been parked in my driveway for the last couple of weeks. It gets hauled away periodically when full, and a new one takes its place. Past the dumpster, I see my neighbor's towering white pine tree. I understand the average life expectancy is around two hundred years, but they can live up to 450 years. There are Douglas firs in my neighborhood with an average life span of 750 years but can grow as old as 1,200 years. The fires that were raging in California a while back have cut the lives of trees there short. Isn't there anything that is permanent?

> By the sweat of your brow you will eat your food until you
> return to the ground, since from it you were taken; for dust you
> are and to dust you will return. (Genesis 3:19 NIV)

I was reminded of my own mortality recently when I heard that Rick Case, a Florida dealership magnate, passed away. I had worked as a consultant for one of his Honda dealerships. He was seventy-seven. I will soon be seventy-eight. As a friend and sponsor reminds me, I am on the back nine of my life. Not much time left to be useful and to do God's bidding. Regardless of when I pass from this realm, I have no regrets. I have made a legal will and testament to be administered after my death, but beyond that, I hope this humble book will be of some use to those who may benefit from it. Is there a key learning from my study of things that bring about emotional sobriety? Is there a personal epiphany on how to better live and let live? I am not too shocked to discover that for the most part I have known all along what to do. By faith and my practice of the AA program, I have been given everything I need to get along better with others without sacrificing any of my own value of self.

Three Key Factors

I am coming to believe that there are three key factors that all of us must reconcile as we seek to live together with our fellow earth travelers. As the diagram shows, I believe we are spiritual, emotional, and rational creatures.

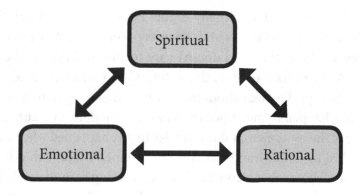

Spiritual Factor

Each of the three factors is essential, but for me, the most critical factor is spirituality. After all, having a spiritual awakening is the goal of every recovering alcoholic.

I was religious before I was spiritual. My parents were instrumental in seeing that I had a church experience with Sunday school, Sunday services, and many times weekly prayer services. It was clearly a priority to them. My dad's meager salary as a factory supervisor of assembly was barely enough for our family of five, but Dad took 10 percent each week to give to the Baptist church. That led to slim pickings to cover the rest of the household needs. As kids, we couldn't help but overhear the sometimes heated "discussions" emanating from the folks' bedroom after the lights went out.

It was clear that my dad seemed to enjoy church activities with the other parishioners. The smiles were not seen so much when he was around us at home. Knowing what I know today about just how hard it was for him to cope, I can understand why he was the way he was. I am like him more than I would like to admit. He white-knuckled his way through life, and for a lot of my life, so did I.

There is no doubt in my mind that he was a Christian and believed with all his heart, mind, and spirit that Jesus was his Savior. His mood swings may have been due to untreated depression or just a sadness that his faith couldn't reach. Later in life, he seemed to lighten up a bit, his mood softened, and finally he seemed more at peace.

My conscious contact with my Higher Power (God) has strengthened over the years, thanks to AA and the gifts of service that bring so much joy. If ever I doubt that God doesn't care for me and protect me, I can look back on numerous miracles where God had intervened on my behalf. It's helpful to hear about the miracles that happen to others, but when they happen to me, it becomes foundational for my faith.

One of the most memorable miracles in AA happened when my wife and I hiked into the Grand Canyon. We camped there with other AA. One of our fellow sober alcoholics had been acting as guide and chef for years, and after hearing about it, it was described as an ecoadventure mixed with glamping. Would we do it? Enthusiastically, we said yes!

Our destination would be Supai Village. Supai Village is the tribal home of the Havasupai people, and it is the only continuously occupied settlement in the Grand Canyon. The village is ten miles from the trailhead at Hualapai Hilltop. There are no roads down to Supai, and everything is either carried down by pack mules or helicopter.

Our guide had arranged in advance by packing in tents, equipment, and food, so we were mostly unencumbered. We had to hike into the canyon but most of the hike was downhill until we reached the canyon floor. We were glad we had physically prepared as the going got tougher the farther we went. Imagine walking in soft sand with heavy hiking boots and a pack. Just about the time our leg muscles started to scream and our dry chapped lips warned of impending dehydration, we found Supai Village. After reviving elixirs of Cokes and water from the General Store, we trudged the last push to camp. The campsite was beautiful with a clear stream running alongside it. It was nestled up to the wall of the canyon that seemed to burst straight up from our site. It was even more dramatic due to the contrast in scale.

Thankfully, because our guide had preceded us, the site preparation was well under way. Gratefully we were able to relax after pitching our tents and taking a refreshing dip in one of the nearby travertine pools. This place was magic. It was one of the most enchanting spots I have ever seen. Every day revealed a new adventure. We explored everything we could: the Native American burial ground, towering blue-green waterfalls, and a network of hiking trails that ended with scenic overlooks or spectacular vistas of the canyon wall. There were numerous travertine pools with unparalleled variations of aqua and turquois blue. The pools achieved their unique colors from lime deposits that collected over strategically placed sandbags and chicken wire that the locals had engineered.

There was even a place we hiked to that permitted us to float in place and let the circular currents give us God's version of "Lazy River." It was therapeutic to reach out and touch the overhanging branches as we repeated the numerous laps. No effort. Pure relaxation and joy. Meditation was the norm. Spirituality came naturally without any work on our part; it just came. This was the closest I have come to having a conscious contact with my Higher Power and not having to wonder whether it was real or contrived. There was surety of God's presence. What a feeling. Genuine rapture.

With each passing day, we started to do less together except for meals and the nightly bonfire-lit AA meetings. One morning another AA asked my wife and me if we would like to explore a hiking path that he had heard about. It was located higher up on the canyon wall. Sure, we were up for it, although we were warned it would require some steep climbing—at least initially.

The three of us discovered just how true that was as we faced the first obstacle. It was a sheer vertical rock wall about twelve feet up. There was a rope hanging down those other hikers had fashioned to aid the climb. Unfortunately for us, the rope hanging down was about six feet long. It meant that each of us would have to use our hands on the rope and our feet on the wall to "Spider-Man" our way up.

It was a struggle, but I was able to get up to the top. My wife was next, and with some help from our friend pushing from the bottom, and me pulling from the top, she made. The next challenge was to get our friend up to join us. He was not a flyweight. He had brought a beach towel, not sure why, but it proved to be invaluable. We used it to pull from the top, and with a combination of the rope and his towel, we eventually dragged him up to join us. This was a strenuous ordeal, but we reasoned that it would be easier from here on.

The climb up to the upper trail was difficult, but once there, it felt like we were on top of the world. What a view. We gained a whole new perspective of just how lush Supai Village was compared to the rest of the canyon. The people of the blue-green water really had a paradise of sorts to call their home. We felt blessed to share it. As we gazed, we couldn't help but notice that a change in weather was likely as there were purple-black clouds forming on the horizon. We weren't sure what direction the storm was heading, and we hadn't been warned of any impending storms. Ironically, we were told about several options to get down off the high trail by a person who had hiked it. He said that we could descend the way we came or climb down a steep descent near the Indian cemetery. Or if we wanted to cool off, we could descend by climbing down one of the waterfalls where we saw kids playing earlier.

As we gathered our bearings and started hiking, we had another sign, or perhaps an omen. We saw a very large Gila monster attempting to swallow a lizard. I believe one of us jokingly wondered if this might be some sort of a sign. We didn't think too much of it at the time; we started to see purple-black clouds on the horizon. We had our swimming trunks on, so why should we be concerned about a little rain? So off we trudged. We hiked with no incident until below us we saw something that looked like a lake of beautiful travertine pools. We decided to get closer, so we traversed down to look. The closer we got to the pools, the options of what to do next became less clear. We decided to wade through the pools. But unlike the pools we enjoyed near our camp, these pools were like walking through marshy swamp. To make it worse, it started to rain.

We decided we needed to get on more solid ground, so we backtracked and were now in the middle of a storm—rain and even worse hail. What to do? Our friend and I used his towel to shield the three of us from the hail. What we thought was a silly thing to take on a hike now seemed like a godsend. It was raining so hard we could barely see the canyon rim, but what we could see were hundreds of waterfalls that weren't there prior. We had to get to even higher ground. Shortly, two separate streams were now forming on either side of where we stood. The streams were quickly growing into rivers. We decided that if we stayed where we were, we would likely drown. We left the spot, just as the two rivers merged, and literally clawed our way higher. Fortunately for us we stumbled onto the higher trail, but now what? We agreed to try to locate one of the ways down that were suggested to us prior to the hike.

We started by looking for the cemetery route. We walked back and forth a bit but eventually found it. All of us decided, however, that in the rain, this very steep descent would not be possible. Our next choice to try would be the waterfall route. We arrived there to find a waterfall all right, but now the trickle the kids were climbing was a roaring gusher. We would be swept to our death if we tried any part of that descent.

We finally decided to attempt to go down the way we got up. By the time we got there, we couldn't believe our eyes. The area we climbed was now filled with huge boulders. Fortunately for us, the guy who told us about the upper trail was now a small figure at the bottom where we had begun. He was yelling at us to start coming down. He told us that he would guide our every step. We were frightened but felt we really didn't have any other alternative.

I want to emphasize that we were barely qualified to hike let alone to descend a treacherous pile of rocks. But this man was a climber, and we did exactly what he told us to do. We were progressing well until we got the final drop. He suggested that we would have to traverse a sheer vertical span by placing our hands and feet in the few crevasses to be found. He warned us not to look down. He told each of us precisely where to place our hands and feet. He spoke to us with a confidence we lacked, but each of us did precisely what he directed. He made us believe we could do what none of us thought we could. And we did it!

I now know that any of the choices other than the one we chose would have been lethal. Additionally, even if we had decided to take the original ascent route earlier than when we did, we would have been crushed to death. I know without any hesitation that God was doing for us what we could not do for ourselves. I believe that all of us were there at that specific point of time to fulfill one of God's assignments for each of us. Miraculously, none of the campers were injured or lost. We found out later that numerous animals had perished.

In the process of being helicoptered out, we could see the enormity of the devastation. It was a life-defining event. We were all so humbled and genuinely grateful to be spared, and before we all departed, we pledged to meet every year to celebrate our miracle and proclaim our gratitude. That promise was kept once. Even this level of experience did not sustain the strength of the original intense camaraderie and unity. Maybe that's the best alcoholics can do—even recovering ones.

My greatest awareness in sobriety is that my wife continues to be my miracle. Anyone who is struggling on her own and still makes time to help others is indeed acting out of love, not out of any sense of duty. There were dark times and still are to this day, but I know God is working through her.

I had been in a hospital for over a week with a bowel blockage. She was not only there for me but talked me through a couple of very dark episodes. When the pain was on the verge of unbearable, I told her that I didn't feel like God cared for me and that I decided that the only way out was to kill myself. She had her own challenging issues, but she sat on the bed next to me and told me that I was not a quitter and that God has always been there for me and would not desert me. Intellectually, I knew she was right, but I admit I did not believe it emotionally, way down deep. I was an invalid. It wasn't just physically but emotionally as well; I was weak, no longer valid, and no longer useful. I don't think I ever loved my wife more than I did at that moment. The pain would subside, but now I was aware that I had been given more than a wife. I had been given a partner sent by and empowered by God. She was and still is literally an angel and my soul mate for life. I am indeed experiencing a miracle every day we are together. I believe in miracles.

Emotional Factor

I believe I inherited my disease and my emotional makeup from my mother. I never saw my mother take a drink, nor do I know for sure if she had the alcoholic gene.

I don't remember much of the early years, but I do remember my mom as a loving and sensitive woman. She sang to me and told me stories. She was a gentle creature. I never heard her raise her voice in anger. While she attended church regularly with my father, I wouldn't call her religious. She had found a spirituality that was deeply felt, and she had a peace and serenity that were evident to all who knew her. And while she was obviously spiritual, it was her emotional makeup that influenced me most. She was one of the most loving human beings I have ever known. I loved her deeply, and the feeling was mutual.

Any difficulty I have had before or since with knowing I was loved or that I was in love was held against the standard of what I felt from my mom. Her sensitivity and gentle nature captured every bit of my being and heart. I never doubted that she loved me deeply. She expressed it perfectly in this poem.

For My Valentine

Will you be my valentine?
I fell in love with you the first time I saw you!
We had a close relationship at first.
Then you noticed other girls.
I was jealous but didn't let you know.
Then one day you left
And I was brokenhearted.
Now my love is a silent sleuth
That can track you
Wherever you go.

—From your secret admirer, Mama

My mother was a dreamer. She would sit at the kitchen table in her robe with her cups of coffee and stare off into space. I never heard her talk about prayer and meditation, but those quiet moments at the kitchen table had to include both. I'm guessing it must have contributed to her serenity.

While there were many activities shared with my dad, my emotional makeup was closer to that of my mom. It wasn't until much later in life that I came to identify those parts of my emotional makeup that I inherited from her. My dad was more methodical and logical, and while I did my best to emulate his persona, it was not a natural fit. Any emotional genes I have were likely passed on by Mom.

Any natural progression of my emotional growth was significantly stunted once I started drinking. Once I started drinking alcoholically, I rarely felt anything beyond anger and fear. I had difficulty getting in touch with my feelings.

Historically, people claimed that there were only the following eight basic emotions or feelings:

> ➤ anger
> ➤ fear
> ➤ happiness
> ➤ sadness
> ➤ interest
> ➤ surprise
> ➤ disgust
> ➤ shame

Ironically the two feelings (anger and fear) I felt predominantly while drinking were at the top of the list. Recent research has grown this original list to twenty-seven emotions.

There are numerous flavors and variations for each, and some of those variants could increase the list beyond twenty-seven. Like many other alcoholics, my emotional state can be reduced to three not so flattering descriptors. I am overly sensitive, childish, and grandiose.

Getting in touch with my feelings is one thing, but placing more importance than needed on some of them puts me at risk of overreacting. I learned in group therapy that I shouldn't "stuff" my feelings. I was told to feel the feelings but not wallow in them. I am now finally learning that even if I am unable to control my feelings, I can control how I respond to them.

My inventory work in AA has convinced me that in addition to "accepting the things I cannot change," I am to "change the things that I can." The focus for this change must be on me and on my attitudes.

*Emotional deformitie*s keep me from emotional sobriety and relational fulfillment. Knowing the exact nature of my wrongs is a start, but being able to interact with others without slipping into bad habits of the past requires me to be *diligent* on how I respond to what others say or do. I must do my best to practice new ways to get along with others. This is particularly true if I find myself feeling angry, agitated, or disgusted.

Step ten challenges me to be able to stay sober and keep emotionally balanced under all conditions. As *Twelve Steps and Twelve Traditions* states, self-searching becomes a regular habit. I can now avoid the "emotional hangover." Instead of constantly focusing on my faults, I can now start to focus on my character strengths. I can now practice my character assets in addition to avoiding my character liabilities.

Love and Fear

I reread recently in the book *Drop the Rock* that there may be only two emotions in life: love and fear. I remember reading that "all that we don't do out of love, we are doing out of fear." Is the opposite also true? Is it possible that anything that I don't do out of fear, I am doing out of love? If so, this may affect everything I do, particularly in my relationships with others and with God. If I am acting out of fear, I am likely acting out of self and am not likely to do God's will or be useful to others. If I am acting out of love, I am in sync with my higher self, and my relationship with God is reflected in my relations with others.

As I reviewed the list of feelings and emotions shared earlier, I looked for, but couldn't find, love. Why isn't love considered an emotion? Many people claim that love isn't just one feeling but a combination of emotions and behaviors.

For me, and many other alcoholics, love can be elusive. With all the behaviors and emotions that come into play, no wonder I've been challenged. Driven by selfish motives and being prone to dishonesty and fear, can I honestly demonstrate all the attributes necessary to form a true and lasting relationship? This is a tall order. The disease drove me to isolation and further away from the people who loved me the most. Many of my family and friends tried to help and were stopped with "Go away. I don't need your help." I may have called the feelings I had for others love, but while drinking, it may have been closer to lust or desire, more like a drive, something to be sated rather than sustained. Even under the best conditions, romantic love seems to go independent of one's will. Only the love of God is perfect.

True love can be a goal, but for this alcoholic, it's an elusive one. I believe that loving requires the same kind of effort I extend as I continue to improve my conscious contact with my Higher Power. It must be sought. I must desire it and value it. Past any of the initial early fascinations, true love requires effort. I must work for it. It requires me to be humble, honest, attentive, and committed. And like my relationship with my Higher Power, it is only possible if I remain sober. The alcoholic must be relieved of the bondage of self. Selfishness and self-centeredness block me from true love just as they blocked me from the sunlight of the spirit. One of my favorite passages in the New Testament is 1 Corinthians 13, where Paul describes the importance of achieving true love or agape love.

> If I speak in the tongues of men or of angels, but do not have love, I am only a resounding gong or a clanging cymbal.
>
> If I have the gift of prophecy and can fathom all mysteries and all knowledge, and if I have a faith that can move mountains, but do not have love, I am nothing.
>
> If I give all I possess to the poor and give over my body to hardship that I may boast, but do not have love, I gain nothing.
>
> Love is patient, love is kind. It does not envy, it does not boast, it is not proud.
>
> It does not dishonor others, it is not self-seeking, it is not easily angered, it keeps no record of wrongs.
>
> Love does not delight in evil but rejoices with the truth.
>
> It always protects, always trusts, always hopes, always perseveres.
>
> Love never fails. But where there are prophecies, they will cease; where there are tongues, they will be stilled; where there is knowledge, it will pass away.
>
> For we know in part and we prophesy in part,
>
> but when completeness comes, what is in part disappears.
>
> When I was a child, I talked like a child, I thought like a child, I reasoned like a child. When I became a man, I put the ways of childhood behind me.
>
> For now we see only a reflection as in a mirror; then we shall see face to face. Now I know in part; then I shall know fully, even as I am fully known.
>
> And now these three remain: faith, hope and love. But the greatest of these is love. (1 Corinthians 13:1–13 NIV)

Based on current events and issues, many folks appear to be angry. I too am often angry, but I have learned that most of my anger stems from fear.

These are interesting times with the COVID-19 pandemic and what was a very contentious presidential election. There have been numerous protests claiming police brutality and systemic racism. Riots have caused millions of dollars of damage with numerous people being shot and killed. There remains a divisiveness and hatred coming from numerous factions who are extremely angry. This is difficult for normal people but more so for an alcoholic.

For the alcoholic, anger stems primarily from resentment and fear. The Big Book also states, "If we were to live, we had to be free of anger. The grouch and the brainstorm were not for us. They may be the dubious luxury of normal me, but for alcoholics these things are poison."

I need to continuously watch out for selfishness, dishonesty, resentment, and fear. And when these crop up, I must ask God at once to remove them. If I practice the Twelve Steps of AA, I will be able to match calamity with serenity. In addition to practicing the AA principles in all my affairs, is there anything else I can do daily to respond to life events with less anger?

There is a likely progression. It may start with a fear that some future action or interaction. I may worry that it may not work out the way I want. And then if the action or event doesn't work out the way I want, I may become burned up or angry. Then, if later I remember that I didn't get what I want, I become resentful. Certainly, I can do an inventory on my resentment and uncover my part in creating the resentment, but is there anything I can do during the time I am angry? Here are some of the actions I commit to take to overcome my anger:

> Identify the source of the anger. Whose problem is it?
> Pause and reflect before responding.
> If necessary, postpone an interaction until all involved are calmer and more rational.
> Be compassionate. Consider the other person's reality. They may be stressed or afraid.
> Listen carefully and hear them through. Let them blow off steam without interruption.
> If the other person is angry, do I understand how they are feeling and how what they think may account for their anger? Own my part in the anger.
> The person who made me angry may be a sick person. How would I treat a sick person?

> ➤ Avoid escalation. Lower the tone and temperature.
> ➤ Avoid personal attacks. Watch the language.
> ➤ Seek outside help if necessary.
> ➤ Forgive and forget.

Rational Factor

While I was drinking, I was not always rational. Instead, I rationalized. I have heard it described since as *rational lies*. I was believing my own lies. I often played the role of victim. I did not accept my part in failed relationships and my resentments grew. I was not entirely honest. I was afraid much of the time, even though I would cover it up with bravado and bluster. I only thought I was an adult. I only thought I had emotional maturity. I mistakenly thought that maturity came automatically with age. I was stuck in my feelings and focused on what you were doing to me rather than dialoging without being enslaved by emotion. Eventually, I preferred isolation rather than trying to get along in social situations. Today I no longer fear people or conversations. Because of my faith in Jesus Christ and thanks to Alcoholics Anonymous, I have a plan for living that has led to more rational behavior.

> ra·tion·al
> (răsh′ə-nəl)
> adj.

> 1. Having or exercising the ability to reason.
> 2. Consistent with or based on reason or good judgment; logical or sensible: rational decisions.
> 3. Of sound mind; sane: wondered if the eccentric neighbor was not completely rational.
> 4. Mathematics Capable of being expressed as a quotient of integers. (www.thefreedictionary.com)

I define rational behavior as behavior that is objective. It is reflected by choices that demonstrate the person God intends me to be. Other synonyms that also apply are analytical, deliberate, sensible, logical, and thoughtful.

Mr. Spock from *Star Trek* fame was totally logical to the dismay and sometimes frustration of more emotional comrades like Dr. McCoy. Although I would like to be able to recall data like Mr. Spock, I do not want to be devoid of feelings. I also do not want to return to my alcoholic thinking that was cluttered with emotions and feelings that led to poor choices and irrational behavior. Here are some of the ways that AA has taught me to be more rational.

Rigorous Honesty

I cannot stay sober without being honest with myself and others. If I expect to live better with friends and family, I must tell the truth. My old bad habit of "rational lying" no longer works for me and the people I want in my life. Even the habit of exaggeration, which I am sad to say has not been eliminated, is no longer acceptable. Rounding up percentages to make my case in a discussion isn't right. Bragging about accomplishments that I claim were solely mine when I know that others should share the credit is not honest. Even humor that uses exaggeration is no longer humorous and needs to be eliminated. I must be accountable for my own behavior. I can no longer blame the words I use and the actions I take on other people or circumstances. When I am wrong, I must admit it. If I have harmed anyone, I must make it up to them and express regret for my actions.

Acceptance

If I look more closely at the Serenity Prayer, I will find some prerequisites for acceptance. Before I can accept anything, I must first be "granted" serenity. To be granted serenity, I must first be humble. God grants sincere requests but only if I humbly ask. The serenity sufficient to accept not only implies that it is gifted, but that it comes because of a sincere and authentic relationship with God. I will never be able to accept anything unless it corresponds with God's will for me. Anything less than that would approximate a foxhole prayer to be muttered in times of trouble. Without acknowledgment of the Almighty, all-powerful nature of God and my place as subject and servant, I will not have sufficient humility to be granted anything. God's will, not mine, be done.

The message in the Big Book makes it very clear regarding acceptance. I need to quit my self-proclaimed job as judge and critic. Someone in the AA program suggested that I need to be hard on me, and easy on others. If I judge myself honestly, I will be better able to be merciful to others. I should look for the good in everyone and demonstrate behavior that reflects the best of my higher self. Acceptance is the price of admission to pay if I am to *live and let live*.

Integration of the Three Factors

The challenge regarding the three factors of spiritual, rational, and emotional for me is the challenge of how to integrate them on a moment-to-moment basis. If there is a gap between stimulus and response when I am interacting with others, just what will I do and just how will I act?

When considering these three key factors of spiritual, emotional, and rational, the growth will happen when I evaluate how I will integrate them when trying to live and let live. The following illustration depicts how these three factors might be integrated:

Three Key Factors

Spiritual

Rational   Emotional

First, the small triangle in the center where all three factors overlap suggests that we experience all three factors. I may experience any of these factors in varying degrees depending on what is happening in the moment. There could be limitless variations.

Looking at each of the overlapping circles above, I am posing the following six combinations of factors, where each factor is listed in descending order of preference:

> spiritual/emotional/rational
> spiritual/rational/emotional
> rational/spiritual/emotional
> rational/emotional/spiritual
> emotional/rational/spiritual
> emotional/spiritual/rational

The purpose behind identifying which grouping is most closely matched will help evaluate individual preferences. Clearly, on any given day or even any time during the day, I may experience more than one category preference. Once known, I may be able to relate better with others with different group preferences. For instance, if my go-to focus is spiritual and yours is rational, I may have to adjust how I relate with you to better live and let live. For instance, I may not relate very well with you if my suggestion is to "let go and let God" when you are looking for a more tangible solution. The following table helps with identifying current preference of factors:

Integration of Factors

If your daily behavior resembles	Then your _factor preference_ might be
> You pray and meditate often throughout the day. > You have strong faith in a Higher Power or spiritual principles. > You are aware of your feelings and can empathize with others. > You follow your heart and rely less on your thoughts.	spiritual/emotional/rational

‣ You pray and meditate often throughout the day. ‣ You have strong faith in a Higher Power or spiritual principles. ‣ You think things through and make good choices based on facts. ‣ You have feelings but do not let them get in the way.	spiritual/rational/emotional
‣ You analyze situations and generate logical choices based on your criteria. ‣ You believe in a Higher Power and pray and meditate. ‣ You have feelings but do not let them get in the way.	rational/spiritual/emotional
‣ You analyze situations and generate logical choices based on your criteria. ‣ You are aware of your feelings and can empathize with others. ‣ You focus more on just doing the next right thing.	rational/emotional/spiritual
‣ You wear your heart on your sleeve. ‣ You place high value on your feelings and the feelings of others. ‣ You think things through and try to make good choices. ‣ You focus more on just doing the next right thing.	emotional/rational/spiritual
‣ You wear your heart on your sleeve. ‣ You place high value on your feelings and the feelings of others. ‣ You believe in a Higher Power and pray and meditate as needed. ‣ Things have a way of working themselves out. ‣ Whatever will be will be.	emotional/spiritual/rational

If after selecting your factor preference you choose to integrate all the factors more equitably by relying more on lower preference factors or not having to rely so heavily on your dominant factor, here are some suggested actions for each factor.

Spiritual Factor Growth

When I think of spirituality, the person who comes to mind is my sister Jill. She passed on earlier this year, and more than almost anyone else I have known, her faith was beyond reproach. My youngest sister and I referred to her as "St. Jill." Half-joking, we would say it, even in front of her, but deep down, we both knew that it was true. She relied totally on Jesus Christ as her Savior. Her faith transformed her. Her demeanor was gentle and loving. She loved her family, especially her grandchildren. I never heard her swear or even raise her voice. She must have inherited it from our mother as Mom was a very spiritual person. Jill enjoyed her life, and even when stricken with heart disease and subsequent heart attacks and strokes, she never appeared to let it get the best of her or let it shake her confidence in God.

Was there ever in evidence that this unshakable dependency on God might have also required a rational approach in her decisions? I'm not sure. I do know that as her disease progressed, she was faced with choices on how to proceed at various junctures. She chose to accept a heart pump to prolong her life. For years it worked; in fact, it worked longer than even the doctors expected. She never complained. She was grateful for the extra time to be with her family and friends. Eventually though the prognosis was to explore heart transplant surgery. Jill was not a decisive person. She accepted everything that happened to her as God's will.

What would have been the outcome if she had decided to go for the transplant option? Could she have had a few more years? Could her quality of life improved? We'll never know as she did not want to take the risk of missing time with her family and opted for the known, albeit inconvenient, heart pump solution. She eventually decided that she was willing to put her name on the waiting list for a heart. She may have decided too late as her doctors discovered that she was no longer a candidate due to cumulative deterioration. She may have died before her time, but she accepted her fate right up to the very end. I miss her terribly, but I am so grateful and proud she was my sister. I was blessed to have witnessed her profound faith. She was a living testament that a life of faith is a life well lived. Rest in peace, Jill. You were God's good and faithful servant.

I suspect that Jill's placement on the "Integration of Factors Grid" would be "spiritual, emotional, rational."

Most people I have known do not rely so heavily on spirituality for their hope and strength. There are the agnostics and atheists who may be spiritual but only out of any solace or solution that may come from logic and thoughtfulness. What possibilities might there be if they or anyone would place a higher priority for spiritual pursuit?

What could you do if you want more of a spiritual focus or you want to relate better with fellow Christians or someone who is highly spiritual?

> Study the Bible; join a Bible study group.
> Move your faith from perfunctory to personal.
> Pray for knowledge of God's will for you and the power and courage to carry that out. Align your will with God's will.
> Practice spiritual principles, and take a daily inventory of how you may have missed chances to do God's will. Ask God what you can do to improve. Rely less on self and more on God.
> Repent from your sins and ask God to forgive you.
> Seek like-minded people to share your journey.
> Pray and meditate.
> Get more active in your church or place of worship.
> Take the Twelve Steps of Alcoholics Anonymous.
> Seek opportunities to serve others. Share the experience with like-minded persons.

Rational Factor Growth

Is it possible to be too rational? I suppose so. I can only imagine what it must be like to live in one's head all the time, depending on one's own rationality as the sole source of self-actualization. And if spiritual and emotional growth factors are not as important, it would seem to me that total dependance on rationality would create a very lonely existence. There are a growing number of people today who trust nothing but the science. They trust the scientists and scientific method and decry spiritual and/or emotional factors as useless, impractical, naive, and even weak.

I asked a close friend before an AA meeting how he might prioritize the time he spends daily and prioritize for three factors of spiritual, rational, and emotional. He said that mindfulness would be number one. I asked him where spirituality would be. He said that it would depend on the effectiveness of his mindfulness. I inquired where emotional might be. He said, "Anyone who knows me would know that it would not apply." He happens to be a lawyer and so it makes sense that he prefers things to be done by the book. He is a brilliant adjudicator and a devout practitioner of the AA program and its principles. I know that he believes in a "spiritual awakening" that will come because of the Twelve Steps of Alcoholics Anonymous. I imagine that his selection on the "Integration of Factors" would be "rational, spiritual, emotional." I think there is a broad slice of our population that likely shares his choice.

What about those who do not have rationality as one of their higher preferences? What can be done to become more rational in your daily life and ultimately relate better with those who prefer a rational approach?

- Accept your feelings and own them, but then try to thoughtfully consider options that are in your best interests.
- Generate choices that will honestly meet your objectives. Be objective.
- Find ways to quantify subjective evaluations.
- Seek the advice of others you trust. Ask more than one person for advice.
- Imagine yourself as another person who is facing the same issue. What would that objective person do?
- Listen actively and intently.
- Evaluate your assessments. Are they accurate? Are they honest? Are they in your best interests?
- Substantiate facts with proven sources.
- Consider cognitive behavioral therapy (CBT).

Emotional Factor Growth

It is hard to imagine being able to sympathize and/or empathize without having emotional sensitivity. Being able to experience the full gamut of emotions is certainly a reasonable expectation. We cry at weddings and laugh with babies as they so easily entertain. Being sad, solemn, and respectful at a funeral is certainly a healthy and cathartic reaction to death.

Have you ever laughed so hard you cried? I have. I can recall times when I started laughing during recollection of a happy time with a friend who had died. Just as quickly, I would end up in tears as my mood transitioned to melancholy or even sadness at the loss of a friend or loved one. My son and his family spent a whole day laughing and crying over the passing of the family cat. There have been books and movies that have given my tear ducts a workout. I have watched the movie *Gladiator* numerous times. There is a particularly wrenching scene at the end of the movie where Russell Crowe's character Maximus had been killed. He is shown in the afterlife walking through a field of grain where he is greeted by his wife and children who run to meet him. I am tearing up as I write this. For me, it was that memorable and poignant. I cry on Good Friday as I think about the torture and murder of my Savior Jesus Christ. I cannot begin to imagine Mary's grief as well as the grief of Jesus's disciples. I can then cry tears of joy on Easter when I think of the unfathomable love God had for us sinners to raise His son from the dead to pay the price for my sins. Pure joy!

I am being treated for major depression. I lived a portion of my life untreated, and it is hard to describe the depths of the despair I felt. Fortunately, there is treatment, and I am now successfully coping with depression. I know the extremes of dark and negative feelings and I am grateful to have been released from that bondage. Thank You, God.

My mother's sister might have suffered from my disease. She was one of the most beautiful, loving persons I have ever known. Like my mom, I don't know if she had any profound religious convictions, but also like my mom, my aunt was spiritually connected without a doubt. I suspect she had a major emotional trauma. Something must have happened in her life that hurt her deeply. I am not aware of all the details. I do know that despite her pain, she always went out of her way to entertain us kids. I never felt any kind imposition.

Having arrived at her home, she would run to my younger sister, Jill, whom she adored, and give her a heartfelt hug. I never will forget that scrunched-up frown mixed smile. My aunt would laugh and laugh and then the tears would come. It was a marvelous, joyful scene with an underlying twinge of profound melancholy.

I am certain that if Ruth were to complete the "Integration of Factors" assessment, she would select "emotional, spiritual, rational."

What about those who would not select "emotional" as a higher preference? What can be done to become more emotionally comfortable? How can you learn to relate better with emotional people? What are things that can be done to have more empathy and vulnerability? What can be done to better use that emotional awareness to live and let live?

- Get honest with how you really feel.
- Practice naming and owning how you really feel.
- Keep a journal on how you feel about daily occurrences.
- Avoid stuffing your feelings.
- Share feelings with close friends and family.
- Avoid "all or nothing" perfectionistic thinking.
- Avoid toxic people and situations.
- Take time to really know others.
- Check your "listen to talk" ratio; listening aids understanding, but telling someone else how you feel will enable vulnerability.
- Take care of yourself; eat well, exercise, and get enough sleep.
- Be kinder to yourself. You will then be able to be kinder to others.
- Learn to love without expectation.

9

Live and Let Live

I desire to live and live well. I am learning to take care of myself physically, emotionally, spiritually, and rationally. I also desire to let others live the life that they choose without judgment or contempt.

Letting others live the way they choose sounds easy, but it can be challenging, particularly if the actions by individuals or groups go against my personal beliefs and values.

As a child, I used to watch westerns on TV, and it was easy to discern who the good guys were and who the bad guys were. The good guys wore white hats, and the bad guys wore black hats. Further distinctions were evident with the bad guys looking disheveled, often unkempt, with untrimmed facial hair. The good guys on the other hand were clean-shaven, well-dressed, and totally tidy even after riding through dust and storm. The bad guys would lose, and the good guys would win.

Going to Sunday school and later church youth groups reinforced the need for loving Jesus and being good. After all, Jesus died for my sins so I could l live eternally in heaven with Him after I die. Why wouldn't I choose to be good? Oh, and the implication was if you aren't good, you will spend eternity in Hades. Carrot and stick. Be good and win, be bad and lose, be good and live forever, and be bad and die.

I must admit that the Baptist sermons scared the devil out of me—up to a point. Succumbing to adolescent yearnings created a dilemma.

Would I surrender to nature's call and rot in Hades as retribution for carnal knowledge, or would I resist even though my loins suggested I wouldn't hold out until marriage?

What happened? The mind kicked in. Rationalization to the rescue. Since the sin of even thinking about sex would mark me Hades-bound, I might as well grab all the gusto I could before my certain descent. After all, isn't this just nature's way of assuring preservation of the species? Nothing could be more natural, right?

I took biology in high school and was aware of the sperm-egg requirement necessary for procreation. I didn't account for just how eager the sperm were to find an egg as I regretfully experimented with prophylactic-less sex. I thought my coitus interruptus prowess would sufficiently delay what I imagined would be a much later in the future realization of the miracle of birth. After all, I was just practicing for this future possibility. Like the ads often proclaim, "The future is now." The result? It culminated in a way too young father and mother becoming parents before they were emotionally equipped to succeed. I can speak from firsthand experience that alcohol delays maturity, and it also defeats the ability to move from emotional to rational thoughts and behavior with any certainty. Add alcohol to a too-young-to-be-married union, and it will end predictably in divorce.

The miracle of this soon-to-be-dissolved union would be a son who inherited my gene for alcoholism. Today, because of the AA program and a mutual devotion to Jesus Christ, we have been blessed with a wonderful father-son relationship.

What does this slice of personal history suggest, and what does it have to do with being able to live and let live? Perhaps, if the book you are reading had been available back then, and I had read it, then the course of history might have been diverted. If I had known then what I know now, would I have done anything differently? I heard this saying from an unknown source that went something like "Too soon old, too late smart!" You could argue that if I had known about mindfulness or emotional intelligence back then, I would have chosen more wisely. I am guessing that my emotional/rational pathway was more primal brain stem than rational frontal lobe.

Then as the years rolled on, adding alcohol to my life kept me shortchanged emotionally, rationally, and spiritually. I was in an emotionally and relationally stunted state of selfish despair. I was relieved from the bondage of self when I stopped drinking and learned a way to cope with life on life's terms by practicing the principles of Alcoholics Anonymous in all my affairs. Is there more to be learned even after I have read the Big Book of Alcoholics Anonymous and completed all Twelve Steps?

Even before the Big Book was written, there were countless religions and philosophies to aid us globe jockeys to connect more successfully with ourselves and each other. And since the Big Book, there have been numerous studies into the realm of medicine, science, philosophy, psychology, psychiatry, and human social science, all meant to help us cope better and live more fully. Because of these advances, those of us who desire to live and let live have more and more tools we can put into out relational tool kits.

Without oversimplifying or being too preachy, I would like to add some of my personal observations and insights that the journey of writing this book has provided. I am fascinated by the marvelous capabilities of the human mind. Our ability to think, reason, emote, create, problem-solve, and imagine is nothing short of miraculous. Based on the research I did for this book, I am particularly eager to learn even more in the areas of mindfulness and emotional intelligence. I am genuinely excited about the many tools and solutions that are available that fall under the banner of self-help or counseling. Willingness to learn the truth about myself and the reality of day-to-day situations will finally permit me to think and act more maturely. All these solutions that help me to retrain the way I think will improve my personal prospects and live with integrity with others. I always considered myself a good communicator, but I now know there is considerable room for improvement, particularly in the ability to listen actively and intently in addition to learning more techniques to use during difficult conversations.

I am grateful to have clarified some personal values regarding my spirituality. I do rely on my intellect and thought process, but there are limits to how much I rely on myself or my mind to get by. I need help, and not just help from counselors or psychiatrists but help from God. You might say that this might be explained by the fact that I was raised as a Christian and that until just recently I had been a member of a church. No, my reliance is personal. I need it like I need oxygen or food. I am truly God dependent. I depend totally on the power of the Holy Spirit. I want a personal relationship and am studying God's word. I read the Bible and follow Christian scholars to aid in my depth of understanding. I depend on the Holy Spirit for guidance and intercession. Because of that dependency, I have come to know I desire more than ever to live and let live. This goal is now only possible if I learn to truly love. I see more and more of what the Bible suggests that I need to do regarding love.

"Teacher, which is the greatest commandment in the Law?"

Jesus replied: "'Love the Lord your God with all your heart and with all your soul and with all your mind.'

This is the first and greatest commandment.

And the second is like it: 'Love your neighbor as yourself.'

All the Law and the Prophets hang on these two commandments." (Matthew 22:36–40 NIV)

I am to love God with all my heart, soul, and mind. I am to love my neighbor as myself. The great news is that God has always loved me. He wanted a relationship and a love that I was unable to return until I got sober. If I couldn't love God, how could I love myself? If I couldn't love myself, how could I love my neighbor? Thank God for Alcoholics Anonymous. Because of my work with the Twelve Steps, I have had a spiritual awakening. I am now willing and able to love others as myself. I have been transformed.

I do believe that a spiritual way of living leads to honest thinking, not wishful thinking. For too much of my life, I relied on wishful thinking. I told people for years that I preferred fantasy to reality, like one of the Walt Disney songs I listened to as a child suggested that "a dream is a wish my heart makes."

Sorry, Walt, but the dream that I wished didn't always come true no matter how much I believed. Should I sue for libel? No, I'd better practice love and tolerance instead and just be grateful that there may be signs of my growing emotional maturity.

I spent too much of my life trying to arrange and control things and people to fit my selfish demands. I recognize that there are many people in the world who thought and acted the way I did. The world is becoming, or perhaps it has always been, a hostile place. People say and do things that are not true and are very hurtful. Regardless of what they do or say, I am directed to love them.

I also am comfortable accepting that "live and let live" does not mean that I have to buy into anyone else's beliefs or behavior. Does that mean I am OK with them believing and behaving any way they choose? Am I able to practice love and tolerance in today's reality? Let's test the premise.

A while back, I heard a cable newsperson claim that there appears to be growing preference for immorality in this country. Is this true? Well, of course it is. People have been rebelling against God and religious leaders for eons. I think of Moses, who was chosen by God to lead his people out of slavery and into the promised land. While Moses was busy doing God's work, many of his followers were melting down gold to create idols to worship. Why would they do that? They wanted gods that condoned and even encouraged participating in "sins of the flesh." They were saved from sin but voluntarily went back to their old ways. God loved them and formed a covenant with them, but they wanted pleasure more than God's love. The apostle Paul later in the New Testament prophesied about this "preference for immorality." Could it be referring to what is happening today?

> But mark this: There will be terrible times in the last days. People will be lovers of themselves, lovers of money, boastful, proud, abusive, disobedient to their parents, ungrateful, unholy, without love, unforgiving, slanderous, without self-control, brutal, not lovers of the good, treacherous, rash, conceited, lovers of pleasure rather than lovers of God— having a form of godliness but denying its power. Have nothing to do with such people. (2 Timothy 3:1–5 NIV)

The newsperson mentioned above went on to pose this question: "What will have to happen for immorality to thrive?" I think I know the answer. God will have to go away, and I believe these people have found a way to get rid of Him. They have decided that some religions are racist and that churches and people who go to these institutions are breeding grounds for white privilege. They support critical race theory. This is borrowed from a Marxist theory that purports social reconstruction. They shame anyone who does not agree with their views. The concept of freedom of religion is just another relic of the constitution that no longer works for them. Christians and Jews are being attacked directly and indirectly. Graffiti and destruction of property are the new norm for some. Groups like Antifa and Black Lives Matter seem to be part of the "new normal." Is this assessment valid, or is it just the paranoia of a conservative commentator? There were events that occurred in Portland, Oregon, that substantiate his fears.

> "Portland absorbed another night of violent protests Sunday that resulted in the toppling of two statues in the city and reports of numerous buildings with their windows smashed in, including the Oregon Historical Society. The unrest was reportedly tied to the "Day of Rage" on the eve of Columbus Day." Apparently the two statues were of Abraham Lincoln and Theodore Roosevelt. Andy Ngo, a journalist who has been documenting the unrest shared the following tweet he received." Shame on all you colonizers! Every one of you that's against Black Lives Matter is (unintelligible). (Fox News)

Antifa clashed with a conservative group in Denver. A person was shot after spraying another person with mace. The shooter was supposedly a security guard with no affiliation with either group. The group Black Lives Matter was supported initially as being a noble response to a horrific racist murder and garnered support to end systemic racism. Who wouldn't want to support eradication of racism? Their underlying motives might be questioned after reading their online manifesto.

> *"AFRICAN BROTHERS AND SISTERS! HERE IS THE PROGRAM OF A REAL BLACK MOVEMENT. IT IS TIME FOR A REVOLUTION THAT IS NON-DOGMATIC, INNOVATIVE AND AGAINST PREJUDICE.*
>
> ***FOR THE POLITICAL INJUSTICE: WE DEMAND:***

UNIVERSAL SUFFRAGE POLLED ON A REGIONAL BASIS, WITH PROPORTIONAL REPRESENTATION AND VOTING AND ELECTORAL OFFICE ELIGIBILITY FOR UNDOCUMENTED CITIZENS.

A MINIMUM VOTING AGE OF 16 YEARS AND A MINIMUM AGE OF 25 TO HOLD A PUBLIC OFFICE.

THE ABOLITION OF THE LEGISLATIVE AND JUDICIAL BRANCHES OF THE US GOVERNMENT.

THE CREATION OF A NATIONAL ASSEMBLY FOR A DURATION OF 3 YEARS. ITS PRIMARY RESPONSIBILITY WILL BE TO FORM A NEW CONSTITUTION OF THE UNITED STATES.

THE FORMATION OF A NATIONAL COUNCIL OF EXPERTS FOR LABOR, INDUSTRY, TRANSPORTATION, PUBLIC HEALTH, COMMUNICATIONS, ETC. SELECTIONS TO BE MADE FROM THE COLLECTIVE PROFESSIONALS OR OF TRADESMEN WITH LEGISLATIVE POWERS AND ELECTED DIRECTLY TO A GENERAL COMMISSION WITH ADMINISTRATIVE POWERS.

FOR THE RACIAL INJUSTICE: WE DEMAND:

THE IMMEDIATE ENACTMENT OF FEDERAL LAW THAT SANCTIONS AN EIGHT-HOUR WORKDAY FOR ALL WORKERS.

A FEDERAL MINIMUM WAGE OF $20 PER HOUR.

IMMEDIATE CREATION OF LABOR UNIONS FOR ALL MAJOR INDUSTRIES.

LABOR UNIONS AND THEIR REPRESENTATIVES ARE TO BE GIVEN EQUAL POWER AS THAT OF INDUSTRY EXECUTIVES OR PUBLIC SERVANTS.

THE RAPID AND COMPLETE NATIONALIZATION OF ALL THE TRANSPORT INDUSTRIES.

REDUCE THE NATIONAL RETIREMENT AGE FROM 66 YEARS OF AGE TO 55 YEARS OF AGE.

FOR THE POLICE INJUSTICE: WE DEMAND:

THE INSTITUTION OF UNARMED MEDIATION AND INTERVENTION TEAMS WITH A SHORT PERIOD OF MANDATORY SERVICE.

THE NATIONALIZATION OF ALL THE WEAPONS, BULLET, AND EXPLOSIVES MANUFACTURERS.

A NATIONAL POLICY INTENDED TO PROMOTE AND FURTHER BLACK AND OTHER PEOPLE OF COLOR CULTURES AND IDENTITIES IN THE WORLD.

FOR THE ECONOMIC INJUSTICE: WE DEMAND:

A STRONG PROGRESSIVE TAX ON CAPITAL THAT WILL BE REDISTRIBUTED AS REPARATIONS TO ENSLAVED DESCENDANTS AND INDIGENOUS PEOPLE.

THE SEIZURE OF ALL THE POSSESSIONS OF THE RELIGIOUS CONGREGATIONS AND THE ABOLITION OF ALL THE RELIGIOUS INSTITUTIONS THAT HAVE BEEN USED TO OPPRESS, ENSLAVE, AND COLONIZE PEOPLE OF COLOR.

THE REVISION OF ALL MILITARY CONTRACTS AND THE SEIZURE OF 85 PERCENT OF THE PROFITS TO BE REDISTRIBUTED TO THE ENSLAVED DESCENDANTS AND INDIGENOUS PEOPLE."

These demands go well beyond "live and let live." Nationalization of industries? Progressive tax on capital? Reparations? Seizure of all the possessions of religious congregations? Abolishment of religious institutions that have been oppressive? How would that be determined? Taking money spent for military and giving it to enslaved dependents? What defines an enslaved dependent?

I heard a while back that a coach from a small university was fired because he replaced a Black Lives Matter decal that someone had put on his office door. He replaced it with a message of his own that said, "All lives matter to Jesus Christ."

Where are those who are crying foul? Isn't this a violation of First Amendment rights? There are those in America today who want to do away with our Constitution. They favor a one-party system and total government nationalization of everything from health to business. They would decide who would be educated and where we would work and live, and we would not be permitted to criticize leaders. Wouldn't that be a communist regime and effectively eliminate the rights of the individual to seek life, liberty, and the pursuit of happiness that our forefathers fought for and our soldiers have died to defend?

My first reaction when I see and hear these things unfold is to feel anger. I know that if I react emotionally, I may not be acting in the best interests of myself or others. And if it leads to judgment, justice may not be served if I am acting on my emotions. As I move to a rational assessment, what will I do? First, I can own my feelings. Yes, I am angry. But is that all? No, there is also fear. I am afraid that I will lose the freedoms that I enjoy living under a form of government that I cannot support. I desire that "live and let live" will thrive, but I am afraid that it might be at the expense of individuals like me. If the "let live" is accomplished at the expense of the "live," it flies in the face of everything our constitutional republic stands for.

Before I get too far entangled in the events that evoke my emotions, I had better look back at what the Big Book of Alcoholics says regarding taking my own inventory.

"Live and let live" will be easier if I "let go and let God." For many of my fellow citizens, I fear that reliance on God is no longer core to their beliefs, but what will I do about it?

I intend to focus on me and on my attitudes. Here's one example: It is my belief that our country must return to God for its survival and guidance, and while becoming an evangelist will not be ruled out, there are actions I can take. I can politically support people and policies that match my core beliefs. I can communicate my beliefs and intentions to those who will listen. I will engage others in conversation, but I will avoid proselytizing.

When do I have to do it? I will start immediately. I will fulfill my constitutional right to vote. And what will I do when the results are in? I will accept the things I cannot change and continue to be the best citizen I can be. The real test is how I will react to the world around me. Can I truly start to wear the world like a loose garment, or will I revert to the single-minded emotional reactor I used to be while drinking?

I must avoid trying to fix my inferiority complex by winning approval from folks who are either unable or unwilling to validate my existence. I suffered from the false assumption that if I just did a better job or had another victory then people would love me. I craved the recognition for a job well done. I wanted to be in the spotlight with an entire audience on their feet, cheering and yelling, "Bravo!" If by chance I got that jolt of validation, I discovered it didn't last. I found that I was seeking approval from the wrong source.

> For those who find me find life and receive favor from the LORD. But those who fail to find me harm themselves; all who hate me love death. (Proverbs 8:35–36 NIV)

There is a story I heard recently that makes this point. There was an accomplished concert pianist who had just finished his professional debut concert and had walked off stage to thunderous applause. The applause grew and people in the audience were giving him a standing ovation. The stage manager was concerned that the pianist was still standing in the wings and not returning to the stage to acknowledge the applause. So he asked the pianist, "Why aren't you going back out there to take a bow? They love you! The entire crowd is on their feet." The pianist replied, "I can see that, but there is one who is still seated." The stage manager said, "Certainly just one person not standing couldn't be that important." The pianist responded, "Oh, but it is. He is my teacher."

What is the moral of the story? Stop trying to please the wrong audience. I may get approval from the entire world, but if I fail to get approval from my Lord, I have fallen short. I am in a constant battle between flesh and spirit. If I focus too much on the flesh or the way of the world, I will lose the comfort and solace that come from God's grace. I must continue to believe that my faith is sufficient to know that I have been delivered from judgment and by faith I will have eternal life.

> For it is by grace you have been saved, through faith—and this is not from yourselves, it is the gift of God. (Ephesians 2:8 NIV)

Because I have been delivered from judgment by faith, I must avoid judging at all costs. Are there any exceptions? What about the when I want to judge others because, in my opinion, they have not earned any grace? Then the light bulb goes on. I didn't deserve God's grace. I did not earn it, but it was granted nevertheless. As such, I implore my Holy Spirit to guide me away from being judgmental. Judgment leads to fear. Fear leads to anger. And anger leads to resentment, which is the number one offender for an alcoholic. If I am resentful, I have lost the battle between flesh and spirit. Does that mean I have also lost the faith to accept God's gift? Ironic, isn't it? When I surrender to the spirit, I am freed from all the pain and bondage of this realm and will be gifted with joy and freedom in the next. For years I have heard that regarding actions in the material world, I probably can rely on my own decision-making capabilities perhaps with guidance from people I trust. When it comes to relationships though, I have entered the world of the spirit. I will be unable to have successful relationships with others without God's help. I must rely on guidance from God.

I never heard my father say an unkind word to anyone he met in public. He went out of his way to get to know people. As we walked down the street in our town, people would invariably greet him. They knew him and he acknowledged all with courtesy and respect, even the people who didn't always treat him well. I would ask occasionally how he could be so cordial to people who weren't as kind to him. He would invariably say something like "Oh, they aren't so bad," and then he would give me an explanation as to why they behaved the way they did. In my youth, I wished he would have stood up for himself more often. Now I understand what he was trying to do. He did not judge. He never pretended to know the underlying motives and reasons for others' behavior. He gave others the benefit of the doubt.

"Do not judge, or you too will be judged. For in the same way you judge others, you will be judged, and with the measure you use, it will be measured to you.

"Why do you look at the speck of sawdust in your brother's eye and pay no attention to the plank in your own eye? How can you say to your brother, 'Let me take the speck out of your eye,' when all the time there is a plank in your own eye? You hypocrite, first take the plank out of your own eye, and then you will see clearly to remove the speck from your brother's eye." (Matthew 7:1–5 NIV)

My father also displayed the ability to grin and bear it. I suspect that he might have suffered from major depression, and he lived in a time where the antidepressants that I have been prescribed were not available. There weren't any psychiatrists or psychologists nearby either, at least that I recall. My father suffered from physical pain as well, but I never heard him complain. He was able to practice what a good friend in AA said about pain and suffering. She said that sometimes we need to "just stand it."

Consider it pure joy, my brothers and sisters, whenever you face trials of many kinds, because you know that the testing of your faith produces perseverance.

Let perseverance finish its work so that you may be mature and complete, not lacking anything. (James 1:2–4 NIV)

I desire to *endure.* I've heard a statement in AA meetings that goes something like "Pain is mandatory; suffering is optional." There are several ways this could be interpreted. One way would be that the effort of getting sober is painful but that the suffering will only happen if we surrender to the disease as opposed to surrendering to the program. It's our choice. The other way might have to do with what happens in daily life. We must endure painful experiences, but suffering from them can be mitigated if we enlarge our spiritual experience.

Pain is a measure of my spiritual progress. It's no longer having to endure the pain of trying to quit drinking as much as accepting the growth pains of moving from alcoholic despair to the serenity of sober living. It may sound overly dramatic, but it is the joy that I feel having risen like the phoenix from the ashes that keep me right sized.

If I am truly *humble*, I may begin to truly love the humans with whom I interact. I aspire to achieve the kind of love that passes all understanding.

> Love is patient, love is kind. It does not envy, it does not boast, it is not proud.
>
> It does not dishonor others, it is not self-seeking, it is not easily angered, it keeps no record of wrongs.
>
> Love does not delight in evil but rejoices with the truth.
>
> It always protects, always trusts, always hopes, always perseveres.
>
> Love never fails. But where there are prophecies, they will cease; where there are tongues, they will be stilled; where there is knowledge, it will pass away. (1 Corinthians 13:4–8 NIV)

What are my intentions now? What do I intend to do to better live and let live? I pledge to bring the best version of myself to all my interactions with others. I will grow my emotional sobriety and emotional integrity in my life, even during stressful times. I will take responsibility for my actions. I will do my best to get along with everyone and learn to respect others without sacrificing my integrity or faith. I will attempt to think less about me and more about others. I will not worry about what other people think about me. I will not rely on the approval of others. I will seek to avoid judging others. I will practice the Golden Rule—wishing for others all those things that I desire for myself. I will work for the happiness of others. I will practice differentiation and let other people be who they choose to be. I will try to focus on the present and not regret the past or worry about the future. I will continue to seek to do God's will. I will live and let live.

About the Author

Doug and his wife, Joan, have been sober for over thirty-six years, and perhaps even more amazing, they have been happily married for over fifty-three years. They celebrate this achievement with credit going to the program of Alcoholics Anonymous and their faith in God.

Live and Let Live is Doug's second book on recovery. The first book was entitled *Spiritual Awakening: Deliverance from Addictions to Alcohol, Work, Shopping, and Lust,* and was written by Will Power (Doug's pen name). That book was mostly autobiographical, and it chronicled Doug's spiritual journey that led to recovery and serenity.

This book has been written to answer the question "What can a recovered alcoholic or any person do to find an authentic connection with others without sacrificing their personal integrity?

God bless all of you who pick up the mantel to live and let live. I hope to meet some of you as we continue to trudge the road of happy destiny.

Printed in the United States
by Baker & Taylor Publisher Services